Arctic Adventures

with the

Lady Greenbelly

Appreciation to
Paul Jance for the map

Arctic Adventures

with the

Lady Greenbelly

by
Kenneth Conibear

Printed in Canada

Canadian Cataloguing in Publication Data

Conibear, Kenneth, 1907-
   Arctic adventures with the Lady Greenbelly

   ISBN 1-55212-441-X

   1. Conibear, Kenneth, 1907- 2. Mackenzie River
(N.W.T.)--Biography. 3. River boats--Northwest
Territories--Mackenzie River. 4. Mackenzie River
(N.W.T.)--Description and travel. I. Title.
FC4194.25.C66A3 2000   971.9'303'092   C00-910938-2
F1100.M3C66 2000

TRAFFORD

This book was published *on-demand* in cooperation with Trafford Publishing.
On-demand publishing is a unique process and service of making a book available for retail sale to the public taking advantage of on-demand manufacturing and Internet marketing.
On-demand publishing includes promotions, retail sales, manufacturing, order fulfilment, accounting and collecting royalties on behalf of the author.

Suite 6E, 2333 Government St., Victoria, B.C. V8T 4P4, CANADA
Phone   250-383-6864   Toll-free   1-888-232-4444 (Canada & US)
Fax   250-383-6804   E-mail   sales@trafford.com
Web site   www.trafford.com   TRAFFORD PUBLISHING IS A DIVISION OF TRAFFORD HOLDINGS LTD.
Trafford Catalogue #00-0106   www.trafford.com/robots/00-0106.html

10   9   8   7   6   5   4   3

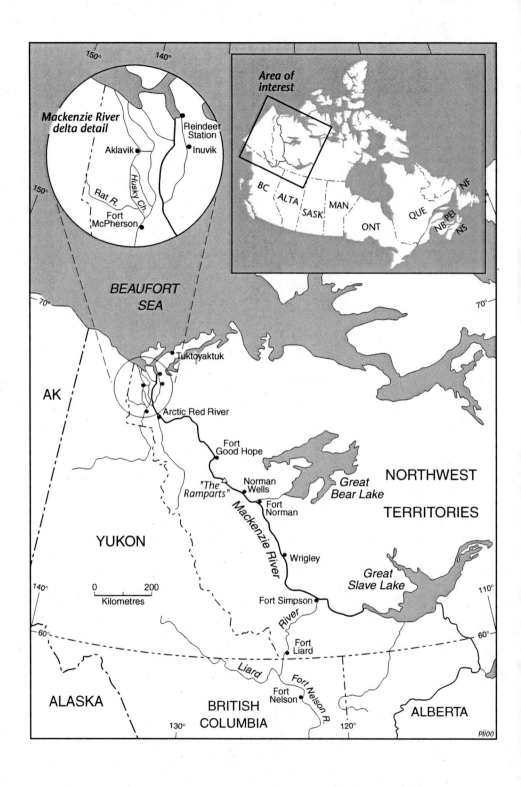

Mackenzie River delta detail

150° 140°

Reindeer
Station
Aklavik ● ● Inuvik

Husky Ch.

Rat R.

150°

Fort
McPherson

Area of
interest

BC

ALTA

SASK   MAN

ONT

QUE

NB PEI

NS

NF

BEAUFORT
SEA

70°   70°

● Tuktoyaktuk

AK

Arctic Red River

Fort
Good Hope

"The
Ramparts"

Norman
Wells

Fort
Norman

NORTHWEST

Great
Bear Lake

TERRITORIES

YUKON

● Wrigley

Mackenzie River

Great
Slave Lake

140°   110°

0   200
Kilometres

Fort Simpson ●

River

60°   60°

Fort
Liard

ALASKA

Liard

BRITISH
COLUMBIA

Fort
Nelson

Fort Nelson R.

ALBERTA

130°   130°   120°

pji00

Prologue

The Birth of The *Lady Greenbelly*

When I first thought of writing this prologue to my acquiring of and adventures on the *Lady Greenbelly* down North, I originally planned to say that, after the War, I had no notion of ever returning to the North. In 1912, when I was almost five years old, my family moved to the Northwest Territories to join my father, a marine engineer, who had been hired by a Catholic Mission to administer his professional skills to their freight boat, the Ste. Marie. Years later my sister, Mabel, and I were sent Outside to Edmonton to complete high school and university, and following that I spent three years at Oxford University as a Rhodes Scholar and another three in England writing about the Canadian North. I was married in England, and my wife, Barbara, and I moved back to Fort Smith in the Northwest Territories of Canada in 1937 where I continued writing. In 1942 I joined the navy and we moved to Edmonton, Alberta, where our home was a vast improvement on what we had lived in during our five years together in Fort Smith. By the time of my discharge in 1946, the rest of the family had left the Northwest Territories and were living and/or working in or near Victoria, in British Columbia. The family still owned a few lots in Fort Smith but the store and home in which we had lived for over thirty years was now owned and managed by someone else. There seemed no reason to return there.

However, three things conspired to draw me back to the North. First, a company near Edmonton which had been manufacturing bombers from plywood during WWII was planning now to build plywood canoes and sleighs, and it seemed possible that I might do a job promoting them in the North, along with some lightweight clothing developed by another company during the war.

Second, I had recently got a letter from a man called Sweet, a retired life insurance salesman who had taken up photography as a hobby and proposed to go on some kind of adventure in the Far North and take pictures, both movie and still. He would give lectures with the movie pictures and turn the still pictures over to me to write a book about the adventure. He lived in Seattle, had read one of my books, and had somehow found my address.

Third, during the War, the Americans had built a road from Edmonton to Alaska, and had so opened a new route into the Mackenzie River which would greatly benefit its inhabitants. I learned of this new route from Navy Stoker Clarence Bell, who joined me in my final work as Regulating Petty Officer in H.M.C.S. *Nonsuch*, which was to discharge, in Edmonton, all seamen and stokers who had originally joined up in Edmonton. Bell had been in the R.C.M.P. before the war, had been stationed in Aklavik, had fallen in love with a girl at the Anglican Mission, had applied to marry her, had been refused, had then explained to his superiors that it they fired him they would find no one else in Aklavik who could put together the engine of the Police boat which he had scattered all over its deck. So he had got married and stayed on, but had eventually quit and joined the Navy. He now told me that he had a contract with Pfeffer to build a lighting system for all Aklavik. Pfeffer was the owner of the largest and most successful store in Aklavik. Further, Bell had another contract, to install an engine in a boat Pfeffer was having built to take his freight down to Aklavik.

"The sooner you can get me discharged here," he told me, "the better it will be. We're planning to get that boat down to Aklavik by–"

I forget what date he told me, but to me it seemed impossible. "Nonsense," I said "I've never known the ice to be out of Great Slave Lake by that time, and from there it's about a thousand miles down the Mackenzie to Aklavik–"

"We're not going that way" he interrupted me. "Pfeffer's getting his boat built right close to the town of Nelson River, and from there we'll launch it and take it down the Nelson to the Liard, and down that to the Mackenzie. So we won't go anywhere near Great Slave Lake."

That was the first I heard of the new route into the Far North. It intrigued me. I got an early discharge for Bell, got many others discharged, in fact got everyone discharged except myself, and for that purpose had to send myself to H.M.C.S *Naden* in Vancouver to get my discharge there. Meantime I had heard again from Bill Sweet. My diary records that on the first of February, 1946, I had received a letter from him, urgent about making the trip this summer. "He seems to be a very enthusiastic fellow" I wrote in my diary, "and he can't write for nuts." In any case, it was a request and a challenge I couldn't refuse.

From Vancouver it was easy to slip down to Seattle and see him in person. He was an older man that I had thought, but was enthusiastic, and told me that he had just received the films he would need for the trip. He also introduced me to Jack Havens, a young, active man who had volunteered to include himself in our adventures.

So I got back to Edmonton, talked things over with Barbara, saw Pfeffer and arranged with him for Sweet and Havens and myself to go with him to Fort Nelson and waited for Sweet and Havens to show up. They arrived in Edmonton during the first week of May, where Bill took a picture of our two sons, John and Peter, of such delight and perfection that I cannot see it without forgiving him for much of the trouble he caused me later.

On May 9th we left Edmonton by train, loaded down with cameras and films, and reached Pfeffer's camp at Fort Nelson on the 10th. The camp was about a mile from Fort Nelson on the opposite side of the river. "The camp" I wrote in my diary, "consists of a horseshoe of boxes with a tarp thrown over them, fifteen feet from the beach." Clarence Bell, who had arrived earlier, and my party slept there. So did Mike Krutko, a trader from Fort McPherson, who had managed a deal with Pfeffer to get his own early freight sent along with Pfeffer's. Pfeffer and two girls he was taking to Aklavik to be waitresses in his hotel there slept in a hotel in the settlement.

A small scow fitted with a V8 car engine turning a small propeller in direct drive made a convenient taxi service into the settlement for numerous evening parties there. Freight arrived from time to time and got landed in Pfeffer's camp, usually unloaded by Jack and me because we were the only ones young enough and sober enough to unload it. And all of Mike Krutko's load was at last suddenly there, ready to go—indeed more than ready to go, for some

3

of his cases of oranges and grapefruit–and some of Pfeffer's too–were going rotten, and we still had to wait for the rest of Pfeffer's freight to show up. This opportunity to rescue the freight and make some money could not be passed up. All I needed was a boat to carry that freight north. Bill Sweet and Jack Havens would follow later on the *Aurora*.

And that is the explanation of how and why I acquired the boat which I later came to call (and to curse) the *Lady Greenbelly*. I've forgotten her precise dimensions, but she was a scow turned up at each end, perhaps 30 feet long, 7 or 8 feet wide, would hold ten ton or more in cargo, and was painted, inside and out, a dark green. I think I paid old Chaunas $1600.00 (and I had to borrow most of that money from Jack Havens) and the idea was that I was to use her to take all Krutko's merchandise to Fort McPherson, and all of Pfeffer's perishables to Aklavik, and there I would sell her for something like twice what I'd bought her for. Everyone seemed to have no doubt that people in Aklavik would be lining up to buy it from me–people who had experience with it, people who had been using it as a convenient taxi for trips, drunk or sober, between Pfeffer's camp and Fort Nelson. For that's what she was, that small scow with a V8 inboard motor turning a small propeller.

What follows in this book is based on real people and events taken from the daily diary I kept of this trip to the Arctic Ocean and back. As a storyteller and writer of what I call creative non-fiction, I freely admit to using a certain amount of 'poetic license' in order to give you a story rather than a diary report. Even so, of all the memorable people and events in the story, only one person was created purely from my imagination. Who that person was, I leave to the reader's imagination.

Chapter 1

The Curse of The *Lady Greenbelly*

L ightly loaded as a taxi, the *Lady Greenbelly* skimmed along the water beautifully, could turn on her tail like a canoe with an outboard motor, ideal for getting around the narrow waters of the Fort Nelson or the equally narrow waters of the miles of little streams that cut their ways across the delta of the Mackenzie River.

But with anything like the weight we expected her to carry, her little swift-turning propeller simply did not provide the power for rapid turning which had distinguished her as a taxi. As we cheerfully headed north with all Mike Krutko's load on her, plus a few items to be rushed to Pfeffer's store in Aklavik, she proved unmanageable in the strong current around Fort Nelson. The river bars were easy to see, plainly marked, but we could not always avoid them. "Mike is piloting and knows the business well" I wrote in my diary on the 23rd, "and I am enjoying it all immensely." But on the 24th I began thus: "Got stuck on a bar about 6:00 last night, on account of a twisted channel where Mike could not swing her fast enough." We ran out an anchor, rigged a four point block and tackle, moved her a bit, and about 9:30 had cold pork and beans and went to bed. "Up at 7:00 this morning, had cold pork and beans, restaked anchor, pumped bilge and got clear at 9:00". That morning we scraped bottom several times, bounced twice on a high rock, took turns steering, sorting oranges that were going bad, pumping bilges, looking for Mike's glasses that had got lost during our troubles on that first bar, and by May 30, "Mike and I are getting a bit fed up with this craft. She's not a well-designed boat, though strongly built. Her engine is good, but it and the shaft should have been fitted into the boat, not merely dropped in." The fact was that in addition to steering poorly she also leaked steadily around the engine, requiring frequent pumping.

We spent another night on a bar on the 25th, picked over Mike's 14 cases of oranges, threw six overboard, spoilt. We then shifted some freight from stern to bow and threw out a sea anchor made from a spare canvas covering. That caught beautifully and dragged us clear of that bar. Joyfully then we started the engine, and found it wouldn't give us any steerage way. We poled ashore and made supper. While we were eating, a canoe came up the river with three trappers in it, all on their way to Fort Nelson with their winter's catch. Mike knew one of them, Charley Jensen. They helped us pull the stern end out sufficiently to get at the prop. Squatting in the water, Mike managed to get it off, and found it badly misshapen by contact with rocks. Charley and his friends then set to beating it back into what they thought was the right shape.

It wasn't: they had turned it from what was a left-turning propeller to a right-turning propeller, as we discovered when we tried it out the next morning. The trappers set off for Fort Nelson, and Mike and I broke out a five horse 'kicker' he had among his gear, made a stand for it astern, and used it to guide us along. We got along quite well for most of the morning, but finally got stuck hard on a sandbar about 40 feet from the left bank. We were there for about an hour when a small boat came down river, and came over to help us. With Mike and me in the water pushing and the others pushing with poles we got her off in about twenty minutes, and then went together in company, greatly aided by the owner of the small boat, an Indian who knew the river well and got us through many difficult spots without trouble. We stopped to have lunch shortly before the Fort Nelson River joins the Liard River, and there I took the propeller off without pulling the boat out. (My diary reports that "it wasn't very cold.") The boat that had picked us up carried a couple of competent engineers. They proceeded to hammer the blades the other way from what they had been hammered the previous night. I filed the blades as smooth as I could while we travelled for many hours, then tried to put it on when we stopped for something else, found I couldn't because the holding nut had somehow got lost, travelled many more miles, now in the Liard River, found a suitable nut in Fort Liard, put it on ("thigh deep this time" my diary says) and we set off, hopeful, as our propeller bit into water with something of her old energy, that our troubles were now over.

They weren't. First the pump would not work well, and the engine soon ran hot. We kept going by packing grease into pump bearings every five minutes. The next morning, now pulling our helpers' small boat alongside, one of the engineers got the pump repaired, but this was barely done before we lost power again and found the drive shaft pins were lost. We went ashore to replace them while having lunch at Mitlaw River, but barely got going again before we discovered the thrust bearing stopper had worked loose. We got that repaired, worked a log out of our propeller, and promptly ran out of gas as we were going through the Liard rapids, with our friends boat tied to us and dependent on us. Fortunately, with Mike's knowledge of the Liard rapids we got through safely–but not without some hard feelings and unpleasant remarks from our fellow travellers. My diary hints that they were not sorry to see the last of us, when about noon on May 29th, we reached Fort Simpson.

In Simpson we searched everywhere for a propeller replacement, found only one, and it was right-handed. We sold two cases of bananas, and got rid of some other stuff to lighten our load a bit, and on May 30th left Fort Simpson at about nine in the morning in a drizzle and a strong wind. The boat behaved better than we expected in heavy seas, merely sending off clouds of steam and muffled roars whenever waves reached the exhaust pipes. Some twenty miles below Simpson the rain stopped and the sun came out. I began making up my diary, and had almost immediately to stop writing because of a noise from rear end. The stuffing box had broken loose from its deadwood, shearing off its bolts as it did so. I blocked the holes and used lag-bolts to replace the bolts. Same trouble a little while later, with two lag screws broken, only one left to hold stuffing box in place; I managed to make that work by jamming a hunk of wood against its head. We passed the settlement of Wrigley without stopping, got another stick caught in our propeller, found a set screw loose in our drive-shaft, and somehow reached Fort Norman on May 31st.

There we had the assistance of an engineer, free, for some jobs: packed stuffing box, firmed up set screws, braced thrust bearing to take some of the thrust which the main engine bearing had been taking, and so on, and on his advice bought a 16 inch 18 pitch propeller, and hauled the stern end out enough to fit it on our shaft. So we left Fort Norman just after midnight of June 2nd with high hopes that our troubles were over.

They weren't. The V8 could not handle this larger propeller. It pinged like a car running up hill in high gear. We pulled into the shore under Bear Mountain, in water still running clear from the Great Bear river, so clear that we could change propellers under water without pulling the stern out at all. At Mike's suggestion we arranged boards to make a platform from the shore to the top of the rudder. At my suggestion, I sat on the platform and got the job done by ducking my head and arms underwater to loosen and tighten bolts, in between fighting off lumps of ice which had made it there all the way from Great Bear Lake. We got underway again about 4:00 in the morning of June 3rd, and reached Norman Wells about noon.

"Norman Wells" I began then in my diary, "is a fair sized settlement—cars all over the place, trucks more numerous still, workshops, garages, toolshops, warehouses, streets of living quarters, a company hotel, a company mess-hall—all clustered around a few pipes numerously adorned with valves—each issuing from the ground in the centre of a pit that seemed to seethe and boil with awesome energy." We tied up at the down-river end of the settlement, alongside some barges. The barges had been deliberately sunk the previous winter so that the water pressure inside would equal that outside, and thus the ice forming would not crush the barge. Now that the ice was melting, a man named Sherwood was refloating the barge next to us by pumping water out of it with two power pumps capable of delivering a full flow through a 2 inch hose. I didn't know it at the time, but the pumps, which I had never seen before, were quite ingenious as they turned off automatically when the water level was down and equally automatically turned on as the ice melted and the water level rose. When we had tied up beside it, the water level was down and the pumps were not working.

Mike went ashore to see about some gas. I stayed aboard to see why the *Lady* had leaked just as much as ever since shortly after we had left Fort Norman. I found two broken bolts through which the water ran inboard happily, blocked them, stuffed the stuffing box, pumped her dry, went ashore, found Mike, returned to the boat, found her dry, and went with Mike to have dinner at the hotel where,

8

for 75 cents each, we got the best meal we'd had in a long time.

There Mike met an old friend, now happily employed by Imperial Oil. He said we could unload our freight onto their barge, he'd use a wheeled crane–a "cherrypicker" he called–it to pull our stern end out, the company welder would make us a new strut and a stern bearing and we'd be away by midnight. Talking all the time, he drove us back to the docks, and there we found the *Lady Greenbelly* completely swamped, cases of eggs, biscuits, and oranges floating and jostling around inside her catwalk. And over all the water in her lay a scum of dark brown oil. It seemed that the bilge pumps emptying the melted ice out of the barges we'd tied along side had started again while we were away and had pumped the water out of the barges directly into the *Lady Greenbelly*. With some neat work by the cherrypicker we got the *Lady* moved inshore and hauled out enough for a variety of pumps to suck her dry again.

"Here" I wrote in my diary, "was the climax of our long run of ill luck–a stroke of pure malevolent fortune, a thing known in insurance business as an 'Act of God'. It was an act directed more against Mike than anyone else. Pfeffer might lose on the 5 cases of Hollywood movie films we carried for him (value $500 a case)–one case was dry, one we lent to Imperial Oil Limited to run off and dry in their projector that night, three were doubtful. But for the rest of his stuff, the actual food value on eggs, oranges, and grapefruit would be unchanged–but Mike had dry goods (children's stockings only), cigarettes, chocolates, biscuits, pilot bread, coffee, tea, and a thousand pounds of sugar in bags and boxes. Much of the biscuits and sugar and all the coffee he heaved overboard as we unloaded by the barge, joking as he did so." (The dried-out, foul-tasting cigarettes we smoked all the way to Aklavik.) A badly smudged note in my diary appears to say that I admired his courage as he faced his losses.

We had much trouble pulling the engine apart to get the water out of it, and much help at that from Imperial Oil Limited mechanics. They also provided and fitted a new stern bearing and they decided eventually that it was less trouble to give it to us and write it off as lost than to sell it and account for the money. They also made a good fitting to hold the bearing in place, and other useful adjustments to avoid the leaks and troubles we had been having. And when we finally got the engine together and could not get it to start they supplied a new set of spark plug harnesses, free of charge.

9

On June 4th we loaded and took off, passed Fort Good Hope without stopping on June 5th, and reached Arctic Red River about noon on June 6th, and Mike's store in Fort McPherson early on the 7th. Mike's store was impressive, largely built by himself, badly mismanaged while he was away. I noted in my diary that he was one of the finest men I've ever known, always cheerful, energetic, resourceful.

I left Fort McPherson at about 12:45 a.m. on the June 8th and reached Aklavik later that day. Stories of the many misadventures with the *Lady Greenbelly* had already reached Aklavik ahead of us, and there wasn't a buyer in sight that would dare to take her on. I was stuck with her!

Chapter 2

The *Lady* Meets the Arctic Ocean

Arriving late on June 8th in Aklavik, I soon found Pfeffer's store and Malcom Macauley, who had been running it for him during his absence. I was soon given a free meal in Pfeffer's hotel, then went to sleep in *Lady Greenbelly* for fourteen hours. The next day we unloaded what little of Pfeffer's goods had survived the hot weather and our various accidents, including the three reels of film that I had hauled out of water after we had left Norman Wells. Mike and I had tried to dry them by hanging them from various places spots on the *Lady* as we traveled to Fort MacPherson. In the wind many of them had broken. When they were shown in Aklavik a few days after I brought them some strange sequences appeared, such, for example, as a furious battle between good guys and bad guys suddenly dissolving into an attempt by Mickey Mouse to feed cod-liver oil to Pluto. In time the local technicians got the sequences straightened out, but in the meantime many of the inhabitants came to see the films again and again, wondering how it was going to work out this time.

On June 9th I thought I'd show Aklavik what the *Lady Greenbelly* could do now that she was unloaded. So I got the engine going, backed out, then started to go ahead, and found that I had practically no steerage way. I had to pole her ashore, explained that she had to have some weight on her, borrowed two empty barrels, set them astern, filled them with water, then tried her again. She behaved a little better then, but I didn't see anyone clamorous to buy her. Perhaps when Jack and Bell arrived they'd be able to help me get her partly out of water and find the trouble. Meantime I'd better just take her out of sight. So I spent the rest of that day buying gas, borrowing a beat-up small canoe, and snuck away when most people had gone to bed, to go rat-hunting somewhere in the delta. Fortunately I'd had a hunting licence for the Territories when I joined the Navy in 1943, and had been permitted to renew it before I left Edmonton.

So I spent a few days all by myself, shot a few rats, and had the pleasure of seeing the *Aurora* go by the *Lady Greenbelly* when I had her tied up in the main channel a few miles above Aklavik on June 14th. I followed, and we were all reunited, and soon busy, Bell and Jack and I unloading cargo, and Bill taking pictures. Bill wanted so many pictures of life in Aklavik, that Jack and I started working for Pfeffer at $5.00 a day plus board, initially unloading the *Aurora*, then stacking its goods in his warehouses.

Aklavik was built on an island on the West Channel of the Mackenzie, with handy approaches to the Middle Channel, East Channel, and Peel River. It could be reached equally by river steamers coming from the south and by the seagoing schooners of the mainly Eskimo trappers in the Arctic. The island was large enough and flat enough to provide a suitable landing for wheeled aircraft. Its soil was pure sand, deposited there by the Mackenzie River over many eons. It had two stores, Pfeffer's and the Hudson Bay Company's, ware-houses for both, and a few individual homes. Between islands across the river there was another channel in which many Eskimo schooners were tied to the shore. All the delta islands were at a uniform height, some four or five feet above the water level when we were there that spring, and normally just high enough to keep them out of danger of being flooded during the spring break-up of the ice–and perilously close to flooding in an abnormal breakup. One of the conveniences of it was that if you dug down a few feet, even in an unusually warm summer, you would come to ice, and could safely store meat and other suchlike goods without danger of their spoiling.

That was the situation at that time, but is no more. Buildings then, of all kinds, had been erected on top of the soil. But as the settlement grew a different kind of building, chiefly Government, began to be added, with concrete basements and other disturbances of the soil. So bit by bit the soil around these new buildings melted and slowly slid into the water, taking their buildings with them. So Aklavik was abandoned several years later, replaced by the new village of Inuvik, a little further up the Mackenzie, well above the banks of the river.

At the time we were there the sun shone night and day and two activities seemed to go on continuously. One was on water; someone going some place in a canoe with a kicker, or more likely sitting in a canoe and trying to get the kicker to start. The other was on shore, playing poker. The head of the Anglican mission in Aklavik one day pointed out to me the collection of schooners owned by Eskimos in the channel across from us and said to me: "Without poker, those boats wouldn't be there." He then explained to me that the Eskimos would go out in the fall, trap all winter, and come back in the spring with their entire catch; would then pay of what they owed the trader; would then buy most of their supplies for the summer; would then probably in a good year have a few hundred dollars left and nothing to do except gamble.

And gamble they did. I initially located four teepees set up in scattered parts of the settlement where poker went on throughout night and day equally, usually four or five people gambling together, some new or freshly wakened man filling in the space of someone who got sleepy or went broke. As more and more went broke the number of teepees so devoted declined, till only one was left, and the players in it reduced to four, to three, to two, to one. "So," said my clerical informant, "instead of twenty men with something like five hundred dollars each they wind up with them all broke except one, and he may have $10,000 or more, and with that he can buy a schooner, which, as is their custom, they can all use whenever its owner is going their way."

The language spoken in the gambling tent was almost entirely Eskimo—a language which seemed to me full of sudden stops and surprises. Jack and I helped unload the *Aurora* with a gang of Indians and Eskimos, of whom one old Husky was the only one we could understand. We made him laugh greatly by calling out "Mukwa" without any idea of what it meant, but satisfied by the reception it got. We had various explanations before the day was over, including "dog-food" and "white man"—which are possibly identical.

There were at least four languages spoken in Aklavik at that time: English and Eh?; Eskimo and Eh?; Slavee and Eh?; and Loucheux and Eh?. The "Eh?" was added to almost all statements of fact, particularly in explanatory narrative, as in "I'm going to put two planks across the gunnels and pile the two by sixes on top of them, eh?" Or "There's a creek coming in on the right side, eh?. and about half a mile below it the channel crosses, eh?" That usage of "eh?" was common in Aklavik back there in 1946 long before it became one of the identifying features of Canadian speech.

In Aklavik many people switched from one language to another as more suitable to the subject being discussed. Once Jack heard voices in a canoe passing by the *Greenbelly* in which one man was telling a long story and the other was trying to get a kicker to start. It went something like this: "Pok muck oop woof prime her lots, eh, Jo, foo wop muktuk..."

As the days passed in Aklavik I got to know my U.S. companions as I had not a chance to do before. Bill, a good, honest, well-meaning man, got into difficulties with the local populace by an excess of politeness. An incident told to me by Bell illustrates the difficulty. The Bells lived above Pfeffer's store, and had a bedroom, kitchen, and living room theoretically their own. The kitchen was the general washroom for all of Pfeffer's employees. Back of the living room was a hall flanked with bedrooms and at the end of the hall a bathroom with a chemical toilet and a tin bathtub. One evening, Bell told me, Bill Sweet approached him and asked whether it was all right for him to have a bath.

"Sure, go ahead, William" said Bell, "but–" and he outlined the various hazards and how to overcome them. Probably Bill did not hear them–he's a little deaf. He came back to the kitchen a few minutes later, in singlet and shorts, and said to Bell "If I could just trouble you for a few minutes of your valuable time, I know you're a busy man, but I crave audience with you."

"I'm no busier than any other man merely waiting for supper," said Bell. "Fire away, William."

"Well I presume you know the layout," said Bill. "You get in the bathroom and take off your clothes, and you fill the tub with hot water and you are just about to step into the bath when a thought strikes you and you look about for the key. Now you, Mr. Bell, are a man of discrimination and tact, and you can tell me perhaps where they keep the key?"

Bell explained that he had already explained that there wasn't any key, and Bill went away exclaiming "Oh boy, oh boy! Great life! Great stuff for my travelogue!"

14

Ten minutes later he was back again, similarly unclad, and with the same approach and preamble enquired the whereabouts of the tub's plug.

"I told you before," said Bell. "There isn't any. Use a little wad of toilet paper. That's all we ever had in the Navy."

"Oh boy!" said Bill, etcetera.

Ten minutes later he was back again, enquiring where he could get hot water, and after going into positive ecstacy over the answer was seen a little later fully clad going down to the hotel with two empty pails in his hands.

Jack is a young man, a joy to work with, a perfectionist—sometimes a little too much so. He's a nuisance at time, always very free with his advice, but at least acting on it himself, right in there with his hands as well as his voice. One day, June 27th my notes say, we went upriver in the *Aurora* to work on some booms of logs of various sizes, big ones for building, and smaller ones for the street lighting Bell was to install. Many of them were partly aground. We tied up near them, and Bell and I went to work freeing them and sorting them with pike poles, and Jack, after shouting to us with advice on how to use the pike-poles, jumped into a canoe we had brought with us, and started tying ends of logs together. Trying to tow one raft, he leaned too far, and upset. He was a good swimmer, but to keep the logs together and somehow bail water out of the canoe he had to straddle several logs until I was able to pass a bailer to him. Everyone enjoyed this incident, including Jack. We towed the logs up to the mill, and there had to sort them out, to leave the heavy ones there and arrange the light ones to be towed back to Aklavik. For that we needed the canoe again, and this time I got in it, to Jack's annoyance, I think, and to my relief. I'd handled canoes long before Jack was born. For a while he shouted at me, attempted to reach out with a pike pole to the bow of the canoe, was warned by somebody aboard that that was a likely way to upset a canoe, laid the pole down, stopped his shouting, and stood and watched me.

When the job was done and I came aboard, he came to me and said. "Maybe if I stay in this country long enough, you'll make a man of me. What you were doing in that canoe was just what I was trying to do, and I didn't know how to go about it." From then on he always accepted my advice—sometimes wrongly. We became warm friends, and so remained for many years after.

In the evenings when the main unloading rush was finished, Jack and Bell and I got some work done on the *Lady Greenbelly*–or tried to. We loaded her with filled barrels in the bow, and used Pfeffer's truck to pull her stern out of water. We found that one of her two rudders had got bent, presumably in contact with a drift log at some time, repaired that, and on June 28th built and attached a new skeg for her, which I reported in my diary as "a fine solid job...I hope." We also filed a little off the edges of her propellor. Then we shoved her in and tried her again. She was a little better, but not enough to attract any offers from the local people.

Early in July the Northern Trader boat *Slave* came in, and on the 4th Bill went on it to be taken to the Reindeer Depot nearer to the ocean, to take pictures of the roundup and life in general there. She had brought several tons of goods for Pfeffer's store, and Jack and I stayed behind to help in unloading them and segregating them for loading in the two large freight warehouses, an old barn (that's what my notes call it) used as a warehouse, an old store used as a fur warehouse, a log building used as a warehouse, and an erection known as a "fishhouse" but used as a warehouse. It was an interesting experience for Jack and me: he shortly got ticked off for bossing some native workers around, and I got my first bit of Eskimo vocabulary, learning that "o-nuk-tuk" means "hot" and that "ky-o-nuk-tuk" means "not hot".

That job done, we worked again on the *Lady Greenbelly*'s problems. We backed her rear end up enough to get her drive-shaft out, found, as we now expected, that there were two bends in it, each about 1/16 inch out of true. We tried to straighten them by laying the shaft over a hardwood block, and pounding on another block above it. Then we filed down the prop again and tried her out. The prop was still too large, but the vibration was not so bad.

The next day Jack filed the prop some more, while I hunted up the old universal joint in case we might find we needed it again. On that day two accidents happened. First, an aeroplane from Fairbanks made a bad landing and broke a wing and a strut but nobody was hurt; second an Eskimo boy was drowned in the channel across from the town. Jack dove and dove but could not find him; his body was eventually picked up by the R.C.M.P. with drag hooks.

Now we were ready to go, but made a deal with Pfeffer first to take a load of coal to Tuktoyaktuk, a settlement on the Arctic coast a few miles east of the Mackenzie delta. Pfeffer had a contract to take a load of coal there in the *Aurora*, but it was more than she could take in one trip. So I offered to take as much as *Lady Greenbelly* would hold. Jack and I got thoroughly black loading on five ton of coal the next day, for which I was to get paid at 75 cents a hundred, or $75.00 in total, on its arrival in Tuk-Tuk (as we soon found ourselves using for Tuktoyaktuk). With this weight in her the *Lady Greenbelly* went down farther than I'd ever seen her before, and took in a lot of water before her sideboards swelled up. We took turns staying up to pump her out from time to time and to negotiate with a passenger for the Reindeer Station who persuaded us to wait until noon the following day. So we pulled out of Aklavik on July 15th–and a few hours later got stuck on a mud bar at the junction of the Peel and one of the channels of the Mackenzie. From there we got towed off by another boat passing by the next morning, and, after some adventure with another log in our prop and some bewilderment about which channels to follow, successfully made the Reindeer Station at about ten on the 16th.

We stayed there several days waiting for a heavy wind coming up channel to die down. Bill had similarly stayed there, taking many pictures and eating with the crew, waiting for another boat to take him on to Tuk-tuk. He was well remembered in the Reindeer Station. We had lunch with the whole establishment one day, and found it frequently interrupted with questions that began thus: "I realize that you're all busy people and may properly wish to use this occasion to talk about your work establishing a successful, and I'm sure useful, colony of reindeer here, and I do hate to take your time with my minor needs, but I would be pleased if you at the end, sir, would pass the potatoes my way." Such requests were given by many, and greeted with bursts of laughter by all.

While we were waiting, Jack and I did some useful work on the *Greenbelly*, putting some caulking in her upper planks, fitting the exhaust pipe with a higher outlet, installing a pilot-house throttle, and taking the engine's pump apart, finding its oil holes plugged, cleaning them, putting it back, and having the satisfaction of seeing the engine running much cooler from then on. We left there on or about the 19th, got stuck several times on sandbars, got off sometimes by pushing with pike-poles, sometimes by going over board and trying to lift the bow free, sometimes by waiting for a favourable wind. On the 21st in the main Mackenzie channel in sight of a small and abandoned port called Kittigazuit, we ran on hard, found we couldn't budge her free by any of these methods, went to bed with little hope except that some other boat might pass and tow us free, woke some eight hours later, and discovered by some boards I'd sunk in the sand alongside us that while we slept we'd moved even further onto the bar. A little back-ward push with poles then easily got her free. We started the engine then, turned her the way we wanted to go, and suddenly both said the same thing: "The tide, that's what put us on, that's what took us off so easily."

That, indeed, it was. For all her faults, the *Lady Greenbelly* had brought me all the way from Fort Nelson down to the Arctic Ocean. For the moment, I loved her.

Chapter 3

The *Lady*, the Whalers and Tuk-Tuk

Soon after we passed Kittigazuit, following instructions given us before we left Aklavik, we turned right and passed through a chain of lakes, deep, with clean water, and genuine pebbles lining the beaches. So we came that day to Whitefish Station, which is the place where the Eskimos make their base for killing white whales. Again this was a clear freshwater lake well sheltered from the sea, with one single entrance. Fifteen or twenty families camped there, on a sandspit which nearly blocks the channel. An Eskimo whom we had met in Aklavik and who spoke good English appointed himself welcomer, and gave us good advice. There would be no more lakes between here and Tuktoyaktuk and it would be unsafe for our scow to go on the open sea until the weather settled. So we had better tie up for the night, with a bow line ashore and something to hold the stern out straight because the tide here rose and fell several feet. So we tied our bow to a drift log firmly buried in the sand and our stern to a bag we'd filled with sand and sunk to the bottom and were in an ideal position to see what the Eskimos did with whales.

One had just recently been brought in, shot and then towed behind a schooner. It lay on the beach, and men and women were attacking it with knives shaped something like half a dinner plate with a grip on the straight edge, an ulu, cutting it into five or six inch squares about two inches thick, and joined one piece to another for a total of about six feet. When these were detached they were hung on a stage, where the wind caused them to turn slowly around, revealing alternately red flesh and white blubber. A little way off was a 45 gallon barrel which had been cut open at one of the rings which divide it into thirds. The smaller portion had been set on the ground and become a firebox for the larger portion set the right way up on top of it. The larger portion had been filled apparently with water, but so many squares of flesh, blubber, and skin had been boiled in it that it had become, to our eyes, a vile mess of fat and guck. One old man tended it, stirring with a hay fork and occasionally dipping a spoon in to lift to his lips and swallow with every evidence of pleasure. All around the stage and the boiler were entrails smelly and greasy, and a little further on a pair of lungs, each about twice the size of a rugby football, and about as resilient. The blubber, we were told, would keep indefinitely once it was cooked. The whales were estimated to run from half a ton to a ton, with some making a full ton and a half.

We were anxious to get to sleep. So we moved away from the beach, used only the weighted bag for an anchor where the lake was deepest, and did not wake till morning brought us the sound of a motor and a voice calling "Hellow, hellow, wake up, white mans!" It was our Eskimo welcomer of the day before telling us that the wind had dropped and we could now safely go on to Tuk-Tuk. He had come out especially to waken us, and was gone, probably asleep again, when we passed his boat on our way out a few minutes later.

We set out for Tuk-Tuk with two small worries in my mind, three in Jack's. We were both worried about the starboard rudder, which had apparently got bumped out of line during one of our adventures on sand bars. And we were both worried about the engine pump, which needed cleaning after filling up with mud on the sand bars. And Jack was properly, and sensibly, worried about running on the open ocean with a heavy load in a mere scow. Well, the rudder functioned well enough, the pump threw out a lot of settled mud as soon as we started the engine, and the crossing was quite pleasant, with a steady roll and pitch only occasionally worrying us till we got used to it. There was a long swell from yesterday's wind, running largely inshore, and a shorter sea following with that day's wind. We shipped no water and hit no bars, left about 3 a.m. and made it to Tuk-Tuk by 7 a.m., July 24th.

We soon found Bill, and woke him, and he was very pleased and much relieved to see us. We had breakfast with him, and walked about a bit, and were delighted with the comments of the Eskimos we met. "Just you two come?" "What Pilot you got?" "How you find the way?" Then the *Aurora* arrived, and was shortly tied up alongside the *Greenbelly.* It had brought the rest of the coal, and about a hundred cases of groceries. Pfeffer had also brought a large gang of helpers, about ten or so, some of whom Jack and I had got to know in Aklavik. We combined forces to unload, dumping coal on the beach below a collection of shacks recently owned by another trader, now sold to Pfeffer–a peculiar collection of three shacks built together (all of different construction and era) one as a warehouse, one as a store, one as a home, but each with its own door and no door between any of them. We unloaded the *Greenbelly* first, ramming her hard ashore, and pushing her further up the beach by her propellor as she lightened, and so made easy unloading off the bow. For once the *Greenbelly* had the best of it compared to the *Aurora*, whose bow had insufficient flare for that use. In both boats Jack and I did most of the moving of coal and boxes of groceries up to the bows, and Pfeffer's helpers took it ashore from there. When the job was done we started the *Aurora's* bilge pump and gave both boats a thorough washing.

Then at last came cleaning the coal off ourselves. We had both worked stripped to the waist and were black even up to our hair. Bill got some pictures of us. Then we donned bathing suits and walked down to the ocean, and were instantly surrounded by what seemed like half the population of Tuktoyaktuk, all incredible–perhaps by our mere swimming, perhaps by our swimming in such cold water. Actually, as it turned out, the Arctic Ocean there was quite pleasant, as warm as I remembered finding seawater around the English coast. Bill got a full film of the whole episode.

Tuktoyaktuk we found situated much like the Whitefish Station we had visited a few days earlier. Again there was a large clear-water lake separated from the ocean and a connecting channel between them–all on a larger scale than those at Whitefish Station. Stores, houses, camps, all faced the inward lake, their backs turned to the ocean. We and the *Aurora* had gone through the channel and turned around to face the settlement for unloading. Tide rose and fell in the lake, much as at Whitefish Station.

The building Bill had got for himself before we arrived in Tuk-Tuk belonged to the Anglican Mission. After several attempts to find

21

a place to lay his head, he contacted the Reverend Thomas Ooma, an Eskimo who represented the Anglican church in Tuk-Tuk and had a shack that would not be used until someone came from Aklavik to carry on the church's work. An Eskimo woman in a tent nearby, with an outside stove, offered him the use of her stove; he bought supplies from the Bay, and was soon happy. So were Jack and I when we saw him there: it was quite an adventure for an old man, a foreigner in a strange country, alone, deaf, with annoying mannerisms and quite cut off in his general outlook from the people he landed among. Ooma was Church of England, Sweet was a believer in Christian Science. Ooma visited him there regularly, and they had some interesting sessions. One evening, in the middle of a discussion of transcendental something-or-other, Ooma found the shack chilly, got up, went out, came back with a small stove and lengths of stove pipe under his arms and followed by half a dozen boys with wood, set the stove up, got a good fire going, said "That's better", rubbed his hands together, squatted on his heels again, and resumed the discussion exactly where he had left off.

The people of Tuk-Tuk were as generous to us all three as Sweet had found them. One day a good-looking and jolly Husky, otherwise unknown to us, gave Jack and me three large whitefish as he came ashore from his nets. We took them up to show to Bill, and he, apparently thinking that we couldn't cope with all that provender seized one and rushed out of doors with it to offer it to the first passerby he saw, who chanced to be the very man who gave them to us.

One of the problems facing us there and everyone else in Tuk-Tuk was how to get fresh drinking water. The lake was a true lake, fed fresh water by two streams emptying into it. But when the tide rose the lake rose too, and when it fell it left sufficient salt to make the water undrinkable. So every establishment had a group of large pails or discarded oil drums which they kept filled as needed by trips over to the outlet of one of the creeks on the other side of the lake. Bill had an arrangement with the Hudson's Bay Company to use a barrel of fresh water which had been left beside a small shack near his for the use of company personnel when one of its seagoing vessels came in to take goods delivered by its river boats. He was to use as much of the barrel's contents as he wanted, provided he left an equivalent amount when he departed. So he and Jack and I used it, and in a few days found it nearly empty. We went over to our Eskimo neighbour in her tent and asked her if we could borrow enough for a teapot full for our breakfast. She obliged, reluctantly, pointing out that her barrel was nearly empty.

So Jack and I borrowed two empty barrels from Mackenzie River Transport, borrowed a ten gallon pail from the *Aurora*, took off, found the mouth of one of the outlets across the lake, tested the water, found it slightly saltish, moved over to the mouth of the other creek, tested the water, found it clean and salt-free, used the ten gallon pail to fill both barrels, returned to Bill's shack, filled the barrel he had been using, and filled our Eskimo neighbour's barrel as well.

It wasn't long before we had a visitor–a small boy from our Eskimo neighbour's tent. Possibly because I was wearing a beard, possibly because I was bending over the *Lady*'s engine, he decided I was the man he had to talk to;

"Please, sir," he said, "My mother she ask me to tell you, eh? it's not right she let you have little bit water this morning eh? and now you fill her barrel, eh?"

"That's fine", I said, or something like that. "Tell her we were happy to do it."

He went, and was almost instantly back. "My mother, she say, eh? she give you little water, you give her lots back, eh? That's not right, eh?"

Again I told him we'd been happy to do it, and came near to adding an "eh?" at the end of a statement that she would have done as much for us.

Again he went, and again he was almost instantly back. "My mother she say tell you eh? it's not right she get something from you eh? and she give you nothing. She like make you pair of mukluks, eh? if you could stay here maybe three-four days eh?" With that he pulled a hand across his upper lip. "My mother make lotsa mukluks, she got not much left her teeth, eh?"

It came to my mind that I'd seen other Eskimo women working on mukluks, and noticed how they'd used their teeth to crimp in the front of the soles, and how many of the older ones had little more than the stubs of their front teeth left. So I said "I'm sorry, but we can't wait long. We go back to Aklavik maybe tomorrow, eh?"

He went and came back instantly. "My mother she say you please

23

to wait three days, eh? My uncle Willie get back then, eh? and he's got a pair of mukluks she thinks might fit you, eh?"

I don't remember how we eventually got rid of that boy, but I do remember that when we pulled out several days later she came running down to the shore, waving to us to come back, and holding out what I suppose was a half-finished pair of mukluks.

Chapter 4

The *Lady* Abets a Gambler

The reason we didn't go back "tomorrow" was because of another Eskimo–a half Eskimo, a man I'd met a few days before, called John Jameson, who had spent the winter further up the coast where he said there was an abundance of timber and of rats, mink. marten, lynx, and both white and coloured foxes. He wanted to go to Aklavik with me, and said thirty-five dollars was the usual price for a lift to there. He also wanted to borrow ten dollars from me so he could play poker while waiting for me and the *Lady Greenbelly* to get ready to take him. I suppose I was the softest touch of any he tried, for I've learnt since that he'd tried one of the men whom Pfeffer brought on the *Aurora*, and then Bill, getting nothing from the first, and a lecture from Bill. It seemed safe enough to me, since he was desperate to get to Aklavik and he stated that he had a credit of $370.00 at the Bay there. He said he'd started to gamble three years ago and won himself enough to buy a schooner, but had lost it in Eskimo Lakes. When I told him now that we'd probably pull out next morning, he asked me could I loan him another $25.00 for more poker playing–and if he couldn't pay it back in Aklavik he'd give me a canoe he said he had there, 16 foot long, bought new from the Bay last fall for $165.00.

At supper we discussed plans with Bill, and found he was in favour of pulling out if the weather was good. I took some planks from an island where they had been abandoned, with which Jack and I improved living quarters of the *Greenbelly*. On the way back I met a man, James Wilson, who worked for the Mackenzie River Transport and wished to be taken back to Aklavik. I agreed to take him if the M.R.T. would give me a barrel of gas. They proved agreeable, and the gas they gave me was a rich red Esso Extra, which soon showed that it could swing our oversize propellor with little pinging. They also provided a box of food as well.

About 2:00 a.m., Sunday, July 28th, Jack and I went up to the poker game, and found John Jameson enjoying a good run of luck. We allowed him one more round of deals, for which James Wilson also got in. John made about $100.00 and lost $50.00 while we watched, and Wilson got up from the table $3.00 to the good.

We took off at about 2:30, found the sea fairly smooth, and were tempted to tow a large dead white whale that we saw floating back to Tuk-Tuk, decided that we might make $25.00 thereby but lose a day and then perhaps be wind-bound. So we gave that up, and arrived at Whitefish station at 5:45 in the morning. Bill had been there briefly on his way to Tuk-Tuk, got only a few pictures of the whale butchering operation, wanted more, and also hoped to get out on a whale hunt for pictures of that activity. That proposition seemed promising when I met Alec Stefanson, an old friend there who had been on a whale hunt the previous day, expected to go again soon and would be happy to take us all with him on his boat. So Jameson went off to gamble with other Eskimos, and we all went to sleep, or tried to. The mosquitos were very active, but I thought I was too sleepy to be bothered by them, and so lent Wilson my mosquito bar. I thought that with my sweater over my head I would have the mosquitos beat, but by 6 in the morning that arrangement made me already hotter than I could stand. Then I tried sleeping in a light breeze blowing over the boat deck, briefly succeeded, and then was awakened by a noise that I thought first was the *Mackenzie River* passing by at a full head of steam, woke, looked around, and saw that it was Bill, swimming.

I talked again with Stefanson, who said he would definitely not be going out whale hunting that day, and might not go the next day either, as his women still had all the work they could handle. So we decided to give up the whale hunt for this year, and to pull out as soon as Bill had taken some more pictures, Jack had done some work on the engine pump, and we could find Jameson and his gambling friends. Stefanson's three women (or I suppose I should say Stefanson's party's three women, for I think there were several families involved, with Alec as acknowledged chief) were busy indeed. They

26

were dressed in men's work pants, with calf-high rubbers, and wore coloured handkerchiefs about their heads; from their rear they looked just working women, Eskimos or white; they worked on the seashore, as often with their feet in the water as out; they were marvellously dextrous in their work; there was no giving or taking of orders or advice; each one knew just what she was doing and didn't bother with what the others were doing (a fine object lesson for Jack, I thought); and I marvelled at the way their rounded fleshing knives cut through the probably tender meat, fat, flesh, and hides turning it from an amorphous mass to the linked squares which become food. Looking at them I said to Alec: "There's a couple of men sitting here who've never eaten whale meat in their lives."

He took the hint, and was soon back with a heart and a square of meat. The meat might be compared to a layer cake, being a thin skin on top, a half inch of white meat next, then an inch layer of fat. I believe the fat is the blubber, which when rendered becomes the "ok-chuk" and is much prized. The white meat is "muk-tik"–and we later found it delicious, tasting something like pork, but not so coarse of grain, and rather like rubber in texture. The skin, which I believe is the outside skin of the whale, is later thrown away–or perhaps used for dog harness and other strapping needs.

When the Eskimos saw us taking these tidbits aboard, half a dozen families came with packages, asking us to take them to friends in Aklavik. The packages ranged from 50 lb milk drums full of oil to a sack of bags made from whale intestines and dripping oil. I was told that all this could be kept in the sun or anywhere we liked: the flies might blow on it, but the maggots would not live. The same was not true of the heart: we would have to cook it on the way, or throw it overboard. We chose the latter.

Then it was time to round up John Jameson. He had done pretty well, and returned to us with all the loose cash from Whitefish Station, two wrist watches, two fishnets, a suitcase, and a twenty-two rifle. At one time he had had four watches, a camera, and a three-burner primus as well; but these had since been lost.

We left Whitefish station at 6:00 p.m., 12 hours after we got there. We found the sea quite calm, and followed it to the mouth of the Mackenzie. There we had a little trouble finding willows set out by the *Mackenzie River* to mark the channel into the river, but made the river by 9:00 p.m. All that day we had our visibility limited by

27

smoke. We tried to reach shore to make supper at several places near the mouth, but always the water was too shallow. So we had cold supper aboard. Jack was with me in the pilot house, and we were both annoyed by the behaviour of our three passengers, who spread their supper on the roof of our engine room and stood up on a two-by-six we had laid thwartwise just forward of the engine room, thereby making the boat top-heavy and so limiting our vision of the channel ahead that, as Jack said, "we had the view a monkey has looking out of its cage." Old Bill was particularly a nuisance: admittedly the *Greenbelly* is a cranky craft, but any river boat is bound to heel a bit when one of the passengers leans his full length over the side to clean his teeth. And, as Bell would have said: "When Bill leans, he leans heavy." We got our passengers off to bed eventually, and Jack and I alternated at the wheel throughout the night, until at 8:30 we landed at a spot we had landed at on the way down, where we picked up a dishrag we had left there (a highly valued piece of cheesecloth, formerly the wrapping, inside tar, around the slab of bacon we had broken open there. At Tuk-Tuk we had seen how the Eskimos use such material for mending tears in canvas-covered canoes.) The others prepared breakfast there, and while they were cleaning up afterwards Jack and I went for a walk along the beach, and suddenly he said to me "Gee, Bear, I'd like to take you up into the Olympic Mountains with me some time", in such a way that I felt a lump come into my throat. Sometimes I get a little annoyed with Jack but he's such an extraordinarily fine man that I always feel I shouldn't.

When we got back to the others, they were preparing a meal on the beach. Bill delayed this procedure by a speech. "There's one important, I might almost say essential, part of our activities on this trip, a part necessary to round out any description of life in this country, that we have neglected so far. It's important to all three of us, and we'll regret it if we let the present chance slip", and so on and so on, till he at last got round to taking pictures of the campfire. Why he should have chosen this particular camp for the many we had made and might still make, I don't know. I had had less than two hours sleep in the last 48, and Jack very little more, and we were both dead tired, and not appreciative of the fact that Bill had knocked off a good 9 hours in each of the last 24–though we were agreed that he was less trouble asleep than awake. However, we managed to pass our annoyance off into amusement. There was a pot of porridge that Bill particularly wanted to shoot cooking and being stirred–and he was so long setting up his rigging that the thing was cooked before he was ready–and he set it back on and we took it off and he set it back on and John took it off and he set it back on and James took it off, all inadvertently, thinking of it as porridge and forgetting it was a subject for a picture. And every time Bill touched it he wobbled the spoon in it or had someone else wobble it, till we had a whole series: "John stirring porridge at camp"; "Bill stirring porridge at camp"; "porridge being stirred at camp over open fire"–and after all this stirring the porridge, when eventually dumped out, proved to be burnt black on the bottom.

After breakfast I took the roll of toilet paper and tore off a couple of yards and started down the beach, and being in a hurry and finding that I was facing the wind I tossed the paper up against my beard so that the wind carried the ends out each side and behind me, thus enabling me to unbutton my pants as I walked. It was a perfectly natural time-saving activity on my part, and I didn't mean it to be funny; but I heard Bill emit a huge guffaw behind me, and Jack said something about "the inimitable Bear". Later on, as I was putting oil in the engine, I looked out the cabin door, and there was Bill draping a long piece of toilet paper about his neck, and heading into the wind, with Jack lining up the camera on him. Off he went, mincing along, calling: "Get ready, Jack!...camera!...cut!"

We spent three hours mucking around at that camp, and pulled out at 11:30. I slept till we reached the Reindeer Station at 3:30. The radio at the Station was out of commission (same at Tuk-Tuk since the last atomic bomb was dropped–probably no connection), and there were several messages they were anxious for us to take on.

We left the Station at 4:30, James taking the wheel while Jack and I slept. I woke at 8:30, just as we were entering the schooner channel, and arrived at Aklavik at about 5:45 a.m., July 30th (running time from Tuk-Tuk thirty and one half hours, distance about 180 miles, about half upstream, the other half divided between ocean and lakes). James, John, and I were in the cabin when the radio masts of Aklavik became visible, and James had to admit to John that it was so and he had lost a bet with him that we wouldn't make Aklavik before 6 a.m.

My first business in Aklavik was with John Jameson. I wasn't going to let him out of my sight till I had the canoe or cash value for the trip and for his borrowings of gambling money from me. We went first to look at his tent, which was erroneously reported by a boy whom we met to be "nearly blown down". It was in fact quite blown down, the only portion of it not on the ground being a small square supported by the stove, which itself was collapsed. We helped him set it up, then walked to a house by the R.C.Mission, where he had the canoe. I felt badly about taking it from him but was relieved when he told me he had three others. It was a lovely canoe all right, a plywood sixteen footer–perfect for me to use if I were to accompany Bill and Jack up the Rat River, as they were now contemplating. Jack and I carted it down to the river, then paddled it down to the *Lady Greenbelly.*

During the next few days she proved herself of some value, going up the sawmill to bring back a load of lumber to be used for building a house for MacAuley. Andrew Carnegie came along while we were getting ready, and for a while we had high hopes of selling him the boat for $2000. He did the piloting for us to the mill, and seemed to like her well; but nothing came of it. A few days later we moved her up to her old beach, loaded sand on her bows, took off the old prop, cut her diameter by about 1/4 inch, put it back on, unloaded the sand, and tried it out. The results were very gratifying: the engine seemed to labour less, and the boat showed some of her old speed at last. The hope of selling her was one of the reasons for keeping us in Aklavik a while longer.

There were other reasons too. We were all three waiting to get some mail, and to send some as well. Jack and Bill were considering going up the Rat river and thence across to Alaska, with me accompanying them part way, and waiting for someone who could give them advice on it. They eventually saw Cliff Hagen, who had been up the Rat five years ago and said it should be easy, because he had made it in nine days, there and back. He drew a map, which looked very reliable to Jack and me. If they were to go they would need a canoe, and they had to discuss that with MacAuley. He said he'd try to see about that, and meantime would we help with the house being built for him.

So on Thursday, the 1st of August, Jack and I began work as carpenters, sheeting up a wall. A very sound job was being made of this house–two layers of paper under the sheeting, and the space between packed with sawdust. We had some difficulty getting the sawdust in after the top boards were laid, but we did a conscientious job on it. The wall was to be finished with ten-test, which is perhaps lucky, I wrote in my diary notes, "for our joints were far from perfect."

The next day a plane arrived with the mail. I had a long letter from Barbara, which greatly relieved my mind. There were possibilities that the plane would take Bill and Jack out to Edmonton, but it seemed unlikely, because there appeared to be a full load of other bodies already booked for it. To wait for its next appearance, on the 16th, didn't appeal to them. So Bill and Jack and I had a conference that evening, at which Bill suggested seriously that they try the Rat. Ever since this trip was first proposed I had been hoping that I might take the others up the Rat, but had given up the idea several weeks ago, feeling that Bill was too old and too inept. When he now proposed it, it was a different matter. His proposition, incidentally, was that I take them up the Rat, as far as I could in the *Lady Greenbelly* and leave them to proceed alone from there. This I wouldn't allow: if they are going up the Rat I will go with them as far as Loon Lake, and then come back alone, in the canoe I had recently acquired from John Jameson. We broke up at that point, and Jack and I went off to talk about it. He let me know then that he was afraid of getting stuck or stranded somewhere up there, afraid that Bell would be a heavy drag on us, afraid that he himself might not be much use, afraid that I was proposing to go merely out of a sense of responsibility for them, afraid that by going now I would lose the sale of the *Greenbelly*.

The next day we went to see Macauley about our plans. He begged us to remain working at his house a few days longer, after which he would see about getting a canoe for Jack and Bill. He was also in favour of my taking the *Greenbelly* back up to Fort Nelson this fall and returning next spring with her and a barge she might push, both loaded with supplies for Pfeffer's store.

While I was shingling that day Ruth Bell came and said she had heard Bill talking to Doug Jones about me. Bill told Doug about what a wonderful fellow I was, and how I had taken a small boat out in the Arctic to Tuk-Tuk. "And do you know", said Bill, "he's got two degrees from Oxford." "You don't say so", said Doug, not understanding this at all, "Gosh, it must be pretty cold up there."

The next day, Bill put the priming coat on the side boards while Jack and I put the ridge shingles on the roof, making a good job of it. The wind was quite strong, and it was unpleasant to work there. When we came to put in the very last shingle, I found I was out of nails, and asked Jack for a few. He reached in his pocket, drew out a handful, picked one that had got a bend in it, and carefully laid it on a board and hammered it straight before handing it to me.

John Jameson made a succession of trips past the new house while we worked on it, each time carrying a roll of linoleum, a bundle of bedding, or other article bought at the Bay. His gambling initially did well there. He said he put most of his winnings in his wife's keeping in the hospital each day, keeping out only a small poker stake for the night's game. If the stake sufficed, we didn't see him. If he lost, he did not go to visit his wife, he came to us and borrowed from Jack or me. Reading my diary over for that time I see that on August 3rd I wrote "So far he has always repaid promptly, with a bonus of a dollar or two over (and our suppers one night as well); but I am just as happy that at the moment he owes us nothing. Last night he made $360; I nevertheless think it may be a good idea for me to go to bed now to forestall him in case he may be on the borrow again."

Then his luck changed. His tent was close to where we had the *Greenbelly* docked. We had seen it being packed with new possessions nearly every day–a set of dog-harness, a toboggan, several more rifles, several more wristwatches, a complete set of china dishes, etc. etc. etc. all brought to him in accordance with bets made sight unseen, and lost sight unseen, by other players the night before. All were delivered with great cheerfulness by the losers and eventually so filled his tent that we began to wonder how he'd find room to sleep in it. Then losers became winners, sometimes the same gamblers getting back what they'd previously lost, and slowly his tent had abundant room for him again. And everybody, winners and losers, were equally happy, full of jokes and talks about "next year". Finally, one morning we saw him and another man taking his tent down, both cheerfully and neatly folding it up, and the other man walking away with it.

Jack and I went to see him. "What happens to you now, James?" He gave us one of those wonderful happy smiles which we had become accustomed to all over Aklavik. "Same as before, eh? I help him before. He help me now, eh? I sleep in same tent–different place, that's all–and maybe I get it back too pretty soon too. Could you lend me ten dollars, small change please?"

Chapter 5

The *Lady* Misses the Rat

For a little while on the morning of August 4th, already a bit late in the season to begin a trip across the mountains to the Pacific, it looked as if we might not get going on it at all. The trouble was Bill and a dog. Jack was getting his teeth cleaned, and Bill and I were discussing buying a canoe from a man named Boxer, and how we'd need to paint it, when the visiting dentist, Lorne Taylor, came to see us, breathless. He had just crossed the river in the Mission boat, and came to tell us that the clouds were massed beautifully to the west of the settlement, and a lovely picture could be had from across the river.

"I'll start the Greenbelly and we'll go over," I said.

"There's a few things I want to see to, first," said Bill.

"The clouds are changing rapidly" said the dentist. "The whole scene may be lost in half an hour."

I stepped out side, followed by Taylor, and in three or four minutes by Bill. Taylor and I admired the view, which even from this side of the river was indeed good, with the cumulus banked below the western mountains, and enough wind blowing to keep the Union Jack taut. For the first time since we returned to Aklavik Bill noticed that the dog which used to be tied to a post nearby was gone.

"The scene is changing rapidly", said Taylor.

"I wonder where that dog could have gone," said Bill. "Mr March didn't take him to Tuk, I'm sure, and Mrs March and the boy—or is it two boys they have or one boy and a girl? None, you say? Well I must be wrong. I always thought they had two boys. Mrs March is on her way to England, and I don't opine they'd take the dog over there. Maybe they shot and buried it, eh? I don't see it around."

The dentist is a very polite man. "I don't think they'd shoot it. Dogs are very valuable in this country. But, you know, I've never seen those mountains stand out as clearly as they are now.

"I suppose they wouldn't," said Bill. "Fifty or sixty dollars each, I suppose? Let's see, fifty dollars each–three hundred and fifty or four hundred for a team, eh? It must be quite an investment for a man."

The dentist got slightly impatient. "The cloud behind the mission is changing to a big tower."

I saw that it was hopeless. "What colour was that dog?" I asked.

"Red," said Bill. "It always makes the best pictures. We have red paint, I think you said."

"No, Bill. I mean the dog."

"The dog. Oh, the dog. About fifty or sixty, I think. Quite an investment. Oh boy! what stuff for my lecture."

The dentist decided he was hungry, and took off. We never did get the picture of the mountains as seen from Aklavik.

On August 6th, we bought Boxer's canoe, and began painting it and my canoe. Bill painted the big one a brilliant red, and while he was at it I started on mine with an old brush, very coarse even when new, which made black streaks on the original baby blue enamel. When Bill was done I took the fine brush he had been using, and went to work without washing it out. The final result was that it looked almost like a camouflage job, blue at base but streaked with pink and red–a pleasing effect, but not what I had intended.

The next day we got away at about 9:00 o'clock, taking an Aklavik man, Albert Loyer, to bring the *Lady Greenbelly* back from wherever we might leave her to switch to canoes. By about 11:00 we reached the mouth of the Husky Channel, making about six knots, towing two canoes. The Husky proved picturesque, narrow, winding, deep, with sand-banks strongly ridged in a dozen or so steps by the differing water levels. On some of its many curves we had a good view of the mountains ahead of us–or would have if it had not frequently turned out too cloudy.

On August 7th, we got up at 8:00 a.m., took pictures, had breakfast, took more pictures. Twice we ran the *Lady Greenbelly* ashore to let Bill off to get pictures of her under way. We began to pass between foothill mountains and about five o'clock came to the mouth of a river, with cabins on each side of it, which accorded with what we had heard and read of the Rat.

We had supper on the beach and went part way up that river that evening. The lower part had steep cliffs on each side, some thirty feet high, banded regularly with alternate layers of sand and clay, with swallows nests punctuating the top layers. We guessed its current to be somewhere between four and five miles an hour, and the river's initial width to be about 15 feet, with very sharp abrupt turns which the *Greenbelly* could not manage without the help of a pike-pole shoved into the shore occasionally to swing her bow free. Bill took on that job and most of the time did it reasonably well for an old man who couldn't hear orders shouted at him. We got along fairly steadily, though we were hung up several times, once right astride a clump of willows which we successfully rode until they wrapped themselves around our rudders. Soon after that we ran across another snag, in the very centre of the current, which carried away an iron we had holding the starboard rudder in position.. This gave us a good excuse to work both rudders over, and we managed to secure them with a short length of dog chain crossed over three times and nailed to the transom. From then on she steered much better, and we had little need of the pike-pole. After a while the river widened, with numerous snags in midstream. By then it was 11:30, getting a little dark, making it hard to see the snags. So we tied up and went to bed.

The next day, Thursday, August 8th, we got underway at about 9:00 a.m., ran about an hour, then came to a place where the river grew to something like a hundred feet across, with numerous snags sticking out of it. We found a channel through it, but it was not deep enough for the *Greenbelly*. With some difficulty we got her nose to shore, where Jack and Bill made breakfast while Albert and I paddled one of the canoes a bit up the river. We saw nothing much, got nothing beyond proof that it was a fair-sized river, that the banks had dwindled to about five feet high, and were no longer made up of Delta sand and clay but of rocks and stones instead, and that there were hills close ahead. So we all four had breakfast together, then set to packing, putting both canoes in the water, and loading them. It was

36

near four before Albert took the *Lady Greenbelly* away and left us there.

We pushed on then, Jack and Bill in the big canoe, and I in the small one, till we reached the first rapids. We looked for Destruction City, where the early prospectors trying this route to the Yukon Gold mines at the end of the last century had destroyed the boats that had brought them down the Mackenzie River and made smaller ones from their bits and pieces. We did not find it; but we did find that we had forgotten or mislaid–Cliff's map, on which it was clearly shown. We made the first rapids, which was the worst we'd met so far, by Jack and Bill pulling on the line and me fending the bows off with a pole–a procedure that didn't work very well, because with me in the bows the canoe ran bow-heavy–though my canoe being tied astern relieved that a little. The next one we tried to paddle up, all three in the big canoe, towing mine astern, but we couldn't make it. We got swept broadside once on that, got ashore, and lined up, with me walking in the water alongside and using my hands and weight to hold the nose out. That seemed to work best, and we found ourselves in agreement that "If it doesn't get any worse ahead–and if this really is the Rat river– all will go well."

We camped about 6:30 opposite a rock cliff on the left bank on which a sharp-nosed and sharp-pointed face of a man appears to have been drawn by nature. Some small spruce trees grew there, and I tried to find some good poles among them, without much success.

The next day, August 9th, Friday, we got off to a poor start. Jack had volunteered to make meals for the whole trip but was so slow and fussy that it was nearly eleven by the time we'd finished. and then Bill had to get out his camera and take pictures of our camp again–the fourth time now. "A complete fake" says my diary,"taken after we were all through, posed pictures, every one of them." We didn't get away until nearly 12.

We made fairly good progress for a while. Sometimes I got a line ahead in the small canoe, sometimes we were able to walk right up the beach with both canoes, all three of us in the water, knee-deep. Some more pictures were taken, including one where Jack and I, apparently working like the devil, let the rope slip through our hands as we forged ahead because Bill had the nose of the leading canoe so jammed against a stump that we couldn't possibly move it. It may turn out quite realistic, but Jack and I let a knot in the rope slip through our fingers, which will be a complete giveaway if it shows up in the film.

Fairly early then we passed what we thought was a big river coming in on our left, which we hoped was Barrier River, but after a mile or so we joined it again. It was then about 3:30, and while Bill took some more pictures I went off on what I thought would be a short reconnaissance, but which eventually took me across twin branches of the river we were on, up a five or six hundred foot hill, and no sign of any river coming into it. I got back to Bill and Jack about six, and there camped and there had supper and there went to bed, with less than three hours of alleged travelling behind us that day.

After supper Jack and I got into my little canoe and went exploring, hoping to find that one of the numerous branches would prove to be a river coming into this one from our right. If we found it, it would be the Rat. For the river we are now on takes a bend and comes out of the south here, which the Rat never does on the aerial survey maps, but the Barrier does. We hadn't got very far before in a hard bit of paddling I let our canoe go too much to port and we passed near a leaning poplar tree, parallel to the water and pointed downstream. Jack grabbed it, and we were instantly swept against it, and filled. It wasn't deep, but one of our paddles and four sacks we were carrying got swept away. We set off after them as soon as we got the canoe empty, luckily found the paddle snagged a little way down. We also found one of the sacks and "didn't worry about the rest". (So my diary reads, and I now presume that they were empty.)

We went ashore and travelled on foot for two hours, and definitely established that there were no rivers leading off the one we were on, on either side, for a mile or more. We saw numerous fresh bear and wolf tracks. And everywhere, climbing out of a sort of tundra, cranberries grew thicker than any I'd ever seen around Fort Smith. and they had just turned ripe, ready for making into jam. Near the river there were also red currant bushes, the biggest and juiciest I'd ever seen. One bush would yield half a lard pail full. And in one small marshy valley we found blueberries not thick or clustered, but so large that they would make easy picking; and they were very sweet. Jack and I enjoyed a few quick handfuls of these natural treasures, and so got back to my small canoe, and from there both enjoyed the bit of rapid shooting we did on the way back to our camp.

The next day, August 12th, my diary records "Rather better today, not great progress, but at least an honest days work." I'd got up just after seven and we got under way by ten. We started off by taking my small canoe down river again, to make more sure of the way we had come. It appeared certain that we had followed a long valley that enclosed a large river and led it into the south, that there was only one place where the Rat did indeed flow into the South, and there was only one river in this area big enough to be the river we were now on. So this had to be the Rat. We had thought that we had covered that area while still on the Greenbelly, but it was clear now that we had not. There was therefore a long way still to go.

Chapter 6

Up the Rat - Without the *Lady*

I began to worry about when I would be able to get back to Aklavik and start up the Mackenzie in the *Lady Greenbelly*–and to worry equally about Bill and Jack in the long journey ahead of them after I left them.

The Rat here and, as it turned out, hereafter, had a current that was too difficult to paddle against, and presented a series of curves that made it necessary for us to cross from one side to the other every few hundred yards to find good footing to walk on while we pulled the canoes with a line. Where the Rat turned outward there would usually be good walking for two men towing the rope with one man, either Jack or me, in the first of our two canoes tied together, using a push-pole, or wading alongside, to prevent the canoes being pulled into shore. That worked fine until the river made another, and opposite, turn. Then the walkers would find themselves confronted with not an absolutely impenetrable jungle of trees, but with trees of a sufficient jungle that they had to lean out and pass the tow-line on the far side of them–a slow and painful business. The simplest way around that was to transplant the towing team back to the other side again, where they would now find good earth and stones to walk on. To get them to the other side I would normally untie my canoe, wind the long towline on its floor where I could keep a foot on it, jump in, paddle across, make a landing, jump out, and pull the other canoe and its two men over to my side. That would require towing a long towline behind me, and where it was running fast the force of the water on it would often cause a difficulty for me to stop at a landing.

On August 10th we ran into that difficulty, quite spectacularly.

The river at one place was about thirty feet wide, had a very strong current, a sharp bend, and a rapids below the bend. I tried to cross with the tow line unwinding from the floor in front of me until it came to the end where my foot would not let it go any further. There I stopped it, and though I had the nose of my canoe nicely ashore by then, I could keep it there only by digging my paddle in. The moment I tried to get myself ashore the canoe would go back again, and I with it. My companions could see my difficulty, and Jack called out something which I could not hear because of the noise made by the rapids. However, it was clear that I could untie my end of the tow-rope and get myself and my canoe ashore, and that they had worked out some plan to get another rope across to me. There were numerous ropes in the front end of the big canoe. Jack started pulling them out and joining them end to end. For that he hauled them up on the beach, ran them fore and aft, knotted two together, three together, four together, gave each knot a good hard thump with the heel of his hand, got them all tangled on a snag, patiently untangled and recoiled them again, gave each knot a further good hard thump, tied one end to a medium size rock, thumped that also with the heel of his hand, and started to swing rock and line around and around–Bill having taken care to lie down in comparative safety in the bottom of the big canoe–and so succeeded in getting the rock clear across the river to fall precisely at my feet.

Seeing me seize the line, Bill stood up, grabbed a paddle, pushed the big canoe with it, and started to paddle, facing the stern. Similarly, seeing me with the line in my hand and the big canoe going away, Jack jumped into it, seized a paddle, and started to paddle, facing the bow. Meanwhile, I pulled and pulled on the line, felt no jerk, no tightnesss, felt instead a limpness, came across one, two, three, four knots, all nicely thumped into place, and then, suddenly the end of the rope, all of it on my side of the river, with no canoe attached to it. Just how this happened, Jack and I were never able to work out. He may have thought that the last knot he tied was the knot uniting the rope he had created to the towline of the boat; or, as I prefer to think, seeing the big canoe take off under Bill's vigorous paddling, he may have jumped in the bow end, tried to tie the end of his newly created rope to its towing shackle, and saw it dragged away by my impetuous pulling.

Whatever the explanation, there they were, my two friends,

paddling like mad, their backs turned to each other, neither one knowing what the other was doing, describing slow circles in the middle of the stream, going down with the stream, further and further away. I prepared to jump into my canoe and follow them down, but it proved unnecessary. Jack realized that something was wrong, looked around, saw Bill paddling like mad the wrong way, and from then on used his paddle like a rudder, and let Bill's work carry the canoe over to my side of the bank. Neither of us ever told Bill what had happened, but listened patiently for many days to his story of how he had got the big canoe safely across the river that day.

We travelled the rest of that day and for several days thereafter with little incident but many crossings back and forth, the river getting shallow, with more and more rapids, some of them so shallow that we had to clean out rocks from the bottom before we could drag our canoes over them.

By August 12th, Monday, we were cheered to recognize the Barrier River, to be sure, at last, that this was indeed the right Rat River we were on. Then we ran into new difficulties, for the river here seemed to have cut itself a new channel recently, for we met a fast current between mud banks with overhanging poplar and willow, many of them fallen in. For about a mile of this stuff Jack and I crawled along outside the trees, waist deep, getting handholds on branches and roots wherever we could, while Bill sat in the lead canoe and pulled on the branches wherever he could reach them. At one place two six inch balsams had fallen across the stream; we cut one and shifted freight to work the two canoes under the other. A little further on we had to cross the river, found no foothold on the bottom, and so paddled across, losing about 50 feet in a crossing of 15, so strong was the current. Worse than that, when we reached the other side, my canoe, which we now called *Scaramouche*, being tied aft of the large one, was thrown against the trees so that she dipped a gunwale and began to fill. My parka was in it, tied to the bow seat, and in my parka pockets were my few cigarettes, some cut tobacco and papers, matches, compass, and watch. At my call Jack came back as soon as he had the big canoe tied, and we soon had *Scaramouche* out and drained. The parka pocket was full of water, but the watch was still ticking. It ran two hours ahead of Bill's time that night, but never lost or gained thereafter–which suggested to Jack and me that Bill had never bothered to set his watch to the correct time since leaving Seattle. We never told him so.

Bill had something else he wanted to talk about anyway. A large log fallen right across the stream suggested to me that we might need to make a portage around it. I suggested it, and Bill suggested that it might be just as well to decide right now whether we were going back or going on. This, he said, would be the last day, by his reckoning, that we could get back to Aklavik in time to catch the plane leaving for the South on the 16th. Also he was worried about my taking the *Greenbelly* up to Fort Nelson, since this trip was taking so much longer that we had anticipated. I told him first that we could make it back to Aklavik, downstream all the way, in two days if necessary, and second that if this trip, his photographs, his lectures, and my writing all turned out as we hoped, it wouldn't matter whether I ever sold the *Lady Greenbelly* or got her back to Fort Nelson for other adventures next year. In any case if it turned out I couldn't get her back to Fort Nelson I could take her to Fort Smith and thence to MacMurray even if I got delayed to late September, and finally that I wasn't prepared to quit at this stage or any time.

So we made the portage . It was 300 yards for the goods, and less than 200 for the canoes, I carrying my little one overhead in the approved, and much photographed, manner and Jack and I hauled the big one up empty for the last 200, in, around, under, and over the trees that sprouted from the bank. Here for the first time we had a look at what the rocks were doing to her bottom. It was not encouraging. It seemed that under her multitudinous coats of paint Boxer and her makers had covered her with a coating of pitch. Red paint, grey paint, and black tar, were all intermixed, and largely gone along the garboard strakes from the bow thwart all the way aft.

The next day, August 13th, we found better going, with walkable beaches, and few necessities to cross from one side to the other. We made evening camp at about 8:00, within about half a mile from a hill which the river seemed to curve around. Jack and I climbed the hill, and got a good view of near mountains and the route ahead.

That night a comparison of our sleeping gear caused us much amusement. Bill put down a large rubberized tarp, blew up an air mattress and put it on the tarp, layed a rag quilt over the two, and crawled into a Two Star sleeping robe on top of them all. He was about a foot off the ground when ready to sleep. Jack used a feather tick he had found near Tuk, with a light Kapok robe over it. I found a level piece of ground and spread my Navy hammock on it, with my very light U.S. army inner robe to sleep on. Bill was most amused by the contrast, and got pictures of all three outfits.

Bill had been more assiduous about taking pictures the last few days. I suspect that until I told him that good ones would more than make up for the loss of my time he was fearful of wasting time to make them–though some of his frivolous takes belied that. Some taken during the last few days might be of real value, but what would be the best, however, showing us all working through the toughest parts, it was impossible for him to take, because he was right in there working with us. He tried hard, but to me he seemed remarkably inept for a man who said he had spent much time in canoes. He was most useful in the middle or tail end of the track line, where he could plug along without thinking. If we put him to guiding the canoe he seemed to run her bottom on every rock in the river-bed, and if you dug a channel through a riffle to make water deep enough for the canoe, he seemed to think you'd made it specially for him to walk on. I suspected that his sight was not much better than his hearing. I was thankful that he's got good, patient, careful, indeed over-careful, Jack to look after him after we separated.

The next day I got up at seven while Bill was sleeping and Jack was doing some urgent sewing of his clothes. This gave me a chance to undertake making our breakfast myself without hurting Jack's feelings. It took me about half an hour from the time to begin mixing the batter to the moment when I got the first pancake out, but I also made the tea, cooked the porridge, and set out the prunes while so doing. Nobody had to sit around and wait, and we saved about an hour. The pancakes should have been poor; for, as I explained to Jack, hinting as much as I dared; "When I'm making pancakes I forget the lumps and think of the minutes going by." But by luck they were good, and I made enough to last us all through the day.

We started about nine by my watch and had pretty good going for the morning, but as soon as we had rounded the bend which Jack and I had seen the previous day, the character of the river changed. Swinging close to big hills on the inside of curves, the channel was filled with large blocks of stone that had apparently fallen from high cliffs recently and had not moved far from where they fell. Some of them still had sharp edges, which are bad medicine for canvas covered canoes. All across the river they were scattered, thick, large,

44

and sharp-edged for half a mile or more. We had no alternative there but to walk the big canoe through the water, one man on either side, the third pulling on the towline, ashore. Jack and I had poor footing in the water, at one moment standing on a boulder completely above the surface, the next finding no footing on the bottom.

This passage was ended by what is the first real rapids we have met on our journey. The rest were riffles, caused by bars of gravel that may shift from year to year. Real rapids, as I distinguished them in my diary, are caused by a break or ridge in the underlying rock which remains in place year after year. These rapids dropped about ten feet in thirty, and gave us a tough fight. They were the first dangerous water we had met yet—hardly dangerous to our lives, but providing a serious threat to our canoes and gear. Hard by them, on the right bank, were two ancient cabins, both with the roof fallen in, and with small spruce or poplar, estimated by me to be between twenty or twenty-five years old, growing up from the floors. I surmised that this point marked the end, or winter stopping place, for some of the miners headed for the Klondike in 1898. A remarkable feature of this small settlement was that it had an outside privy, the first I could ever recall seeing for a wintering place away from a settlement. The privy, consisting of a pole frame on which canvas had probably been tacked, was in much better preservation than the cabins.

A little further upriver we made camp for the night, on the right bank, opposite high cliffs on the left bank. There was a smoother camping place on the left bank, but we avoided it for fear of the possibility of rocks falling during the night. While we were camped a small slip of sand did occur, originating perhaps 200 feet up, accumulating as it fell and ceasing at the water's edge with a large pother of dust, some of which blew over to our side as we camped. "Great movie material," said Bill, and went on with his eating. Jack and I considered the possibility of starting another landslip with a shot from his rifle in the morning when Bill would have his camera set up, but when we had a burst of thunder during the night that shook the ground under us but did not produce any land slips, we gave that up.

Great piles of sand lay at the foot of all the cliffs, smooth and solid, looking like buttresses thrown against them to keep them from falling. Much of it was hard, but some made a grey sandstone so soft that you could work the surface away with your bare hand.

Sometime during the night I was wakened by two terrific crashes of thunder and told myself that there was a 99 and 9/10th chance of heavy rain soon. I was in a mood, however, to regard the 1/10th chance hopefully, and remained where I was. The rain came soon enough, and I protected myself by taking down my mosquito bar and spreading my tarp and slicker over myself and my goods. Luckily there were spruce near the campsite and I had cut some for my bed, which now helped to keep me and my gear off the ground. Bill and Jack thrashed around, got a tarp over themselves, and eventually, between rains, set up Bill's tent. We all slept and rested till about noon, when, the rain easing off, Bill got up and made porridge.

The rain continuing, we decided to spend another hour at that camp, and later, for the same cause, changed the one hour to all day. It was a lovely spot, and I was reluctant to leave it without Bill's getting a good picture of it–but the light, as usual, was not right for picture taking. Nor was it right for travel, for we found it unpleasant enough being continuously wet from the waist down without getting continuously wet from the waist up as well.

On that day I made a discovery which should go into the notebook of all travellers in the woods. It was that by backing a single sheet of toilet-paper with a large leaf you can get the same results as if you backed it with another sheet. This discovery I made public to our small company, and had the pleasure of seeing it as a means of relieving an imminent shortage in our supplies. Jack and I pick enough fresh berries to ensure that our bowels move freely.

There was another problem I wished I could resolve as readily. My heavy blue socks shrank continuously as a result of my continual wading. To save ruining them all, I stuck to one pair, drying them out each night (if it wasn't raining), and putting the same pair on each morning. This pair no longer made any pretence of reaching to the tops of my boots, but that no longer mattered, because my boots had now got sufficiently worn, or my skin sufficiently hardened, to prevent chafing about my ankles. The difficulty that overtook me in this period was that I could barely get the socks on at all. One was particularly troublesome: its heel barely reached the ball of my foot, and its top barely rounded the curve of my heel. When I had taken my boot off recently, there was the insole squeezed between sock and tongue of boot, with one frayed end out and gasping for breath. What

46

I did in an attempt to cure that was to put heavy stones in the tips of my socks and swing them violently about my head by the tops. I thought that if I could keep that up till they were completely dry, they'd return to their proper shape and I'd have the problem licked. But it rained, and rained, and the best I could do was to swing them a while, then hang them to trees with the rocks still in them while I slept. Another problem was the soles of our boots. The tread was long gone off mine and it was difficult to keep my footing on wet rocks. Jack's were slightly better, but he was beginning to have the same trouble. Bill, with loggers, can manage a little better; but the hobnails in them were also wearing away.

At sometime during that continuous rain I dug up an old empty four-gallon can that I found by an old camp in the bush and rigged it up for an oven to cook baking powder biscuits. I got two big flat stones, set them up on their long edges, put the can crosswise on them, lit a big fire between them, laid about two inches of fine stones in the can, made my dough, put seven little dabs on a plate, found the plate was too big for the can, transferred them to a smaller plate, put that in, watched my cooking rise and turn brown, and was just beginning to wonder how I'd get the plate out without burning my fingers, when the stove solved that problem for me, by exploding. I mean that literally: one of the rocks simply flew to pieces, throwing my plate full of small rocks and biscuits two feet to one side, knocking the other rock over, and scattering charcoal and ashes in all directions. Later I picked up one piece of the rock, at least 3 lbs in weight, 25 feet away. It appeared porous, and I surmised that it was full of water, which had turned to steam, and so exploded. I found my biscuits, nicely cooked and undamaged, but my batter and my open tin of lard were covered with ashes. I got two round granite rocks, started up again, setting the can on an angle between them, which was the only way it would fit, and which also allowed me to use the frying pan, which would give me the advantage of a handle. This worked very well: the first few batches required a lot of wood in the fire to bake them; but once the big rocks got heated I found I was burning my cakes top and bottom if I didn't watch them carefully. I cooked enough to last us for a few days.

August 14th, Wednesday. We made it about two miles further on. We all had good intentions of making an early start and going a long way, but again the weather beat us. It was raining when I woke at seven, and I was getting a little wet from a hole that had developed between my hammock and my slicker. It was not bad, merely making wet a small portion of my robe, one sock, and a shirt. For once, I did not sweat in my little robe. There had been some snow with the rain, and the hills were touched with it that morning. The mountains then visible to the west ahead of us had become a glossy white. We made a leisurely breakfast and sat around for an hour or so, for it looked as if it might begin to rain heavily at any moment. We started at about two and travelled till after six, helped considerably by a 12 inch rise in the water, and impeded by its muddiness, which made it hard to see the stones on the bottom in the shallow places.

For fear of rising water we camped on a bank about three feet above the river level. We found it by far the best place yet, with moss underneath and both dry and green spruce plentiful. There were also numerous blueberries around us. Some appeared to be of the same variety I had seen elsewhere. Others were larger and more elongated, almost flat on two sides, and slightly swollen towards the end. These did not grow in clusters, but tasted quite like those that did. We quickly picked enough to provide the dessert for our supper.

There seemed a serious prospect that Jack and Bill would run short of food before they reached Fort Yukon. We had not planned on being so long on the Rat and we had expected to get more food from the country. We had not seen a duck since we left the Husky, or any other edible meat. Fishing is a failure so far: Bill had said that no self-respecting fish would live in the dirty water we had come through. Jack and I told him that we didn't care whether the fish was self-respecting or not: as long as they had fins and scales we would eat them. We finally persuaded him to try his hooks and lines in the rapids near the falling cliff; he got nothing, and we feared that we might have trouble getting him to try them when the conditions were better. He seemed to go on unperturbed by the imminent danger of food shortages. I slept under my overturned canoe that night, very comfortably.

The 15th started badly. We worked our way through some rather tough bush along the bank we were on and came to a fast-running rapids with some big boulders. I was ashore with the line, getting it around the point above the rapids, Jack was ashore ahead of me, and Bill was in the lead canoe, with a pole which he had been using quite successfully in the lower reach below the rapids. I got my line around the point and started to follow it back. and saw that Bill was trying to take the canoe up the rapids with the pole. He was already part way, but didn't have a chance of getting up the rapids, because his weight in front had made the canoe bow-heavy and when it hit the rapids it would almost certainly swamp. And so it happened: the nose lurched sidewise, throwing up white water, the whole boat shot sidewise, and water started to lap over the gunwales. Fortunately. I had lots of line behind me, and could let it out gradually till I came to its end. Then by running down the beach, tumbling and thrashing among heavy rocks, moving a little slower than the canoe, I gradually got her head around. By then Jack had joined me, and we soon had her stopped and were able to bring her to shore. It looked as if Bill thought he was on his own at that point, for he had dropped the pole and was plying a paddle very vigorously–in the right direction this time–till the nose touched shore. The canoe had taken very little water, and we got through the incident very luckily. We had lost a pole, and Bill had gained an experience that should be useful to him. He seemed to have realized that this near-accident was his own fault.

Soon after that we had to make about four hundred yards along a shore where the water was very fast and too deep to wade in, and the trees overhung. It took us about two hours to accomplish that, had lunch, and then had good going till we came, at about eight p.m., to a caribou hunting camp on the right hand shore. Rather, perhaps, it should be called a caribou dressing camp. A couple of acres were practically covered with caribou skins and caribou hair–rather whiter than that of the skins I'd seen around Fort Smith. A couple of meat caches, and a few traps and numerous empty tin cans and a general messiness made up the rest of the camp. Bill decided that he wanted a picture of it in the morning; so Jack and I were glad enough to empty the canoes of our night gear and ready food so that we could run them nearly empty through a vicious little bit of water near the camp. I had a lovely soft mossy bed under my canoe that night, marred only by the fact that I had to scrape out a lot of old dog manure before I could use it.

On August 16, Friday, we started off taking pictures and looking at the big canoe turned over on shore. We found two rips and one hole in the canvas, and mended them by heating stones in our fire, melting tar off a slab of Sealtite Bacon and rubbing the tar into the canvas with the hot stones. I hoped it would work (as indeed it did), and Bill thought it was very good movie material, and took many pictures–some of which Jack and I thought would make a good advertisement for Swift's Sealtite Bacon. From the moment I looked at the water in the morning I knew beyond doubt that we were near the Barriers River, for the water on the far shore was muddy and on our shore was fairly clean. (My diary notes make no mention that this was the third time we had reached the Barrier River.) On rivers of this size and this amount of disturbance in rapids their waters must become mixed very early. So a muddy river must be coming in just a short distance away. The size of the caribou dressing site had intimated much the same thing: hunters coming from two valleys had been meeting here. The Barrier River is the biggest tributary of the Rat, and has often been mistaken for it by parties coming up the river, as we were doing.

We found lovely scenery here near the junction of the rivers. The view of mountains up the valley of the Rat was one of the most beautiful I'd ever seen. Bill got good picture coverage of it. We plugged along all of a short day, encouraged by knowing just where we were and by the belief that within a few miles it would get easier, helped by having the clear water of the Rat proper, but aware of its coldness and disappointed by its shortage of beaches to walk on. "To put it generally", my diary recorded, "along the shore there were beaches were the going was good, and in between there were sons-of-beaches. Where the water is reasonably slack, or where it is not over a couple of feet deep, these sons-of-beaches (what is the correct plural?) were not troublesome. Where the water is deep and the current fast, they are far more nuisance than a rapids, and take more time to negotiate and are as dangerous. Where rapids and overhanging or fallen trees and a wooded shore combine, you have a condition which can fairly be described as impassable. In such places you must either portage or cross to the other shore."

We made camp early that night, happening to find a delightful place within sight of a canyon up ahead. I at once set up our four-gallon tin on two big stones and cooked bannock all evening.

On August the 17th (Saturday) we got off to a late start largely because Bill wanted more pictures. We soon got into the canyon, where Jack and I wrestled our two canoes through two little rapids and some easy riffles, while Bill clambered through the bush and over the rocks, taking pictures. I hoped they were good, and would

50

contrast the difference in size between the hills and ourselves. The canyon was nevertheless scenically disappointing, though satisfactory for travelling. At no place did the cliffs rise from both sides of the river at once, and nowhere were they more than a couple of hundred feet high. The colours in the rocks, however, were wonderful, mostly red and purple, but with all other colours represented.

Immediately above the canyon the nature of the river changed, with round gravel beaches, gravel riffles, and water between the riffles slow enough at times to allow us to paddle upstream. We worked till seven, then camped, and while Jack made supper, I shot a rabbit, and located a creek flowing in, which definitely set our place on the map.

So going for the next few days we got within about fifteen miles of Loon Lake on August 20, weary and disappointed. Here we were, two weeks gone from Aklavik, and three days past the head of the canyon, where we had been told that the rest was easy going, we found that the river was smaller and we had mountains each side of us, but the going was just as tough as we had already been through. There were no more rapids, but numerous riffles, and more snags than before, more trees fallen across, more trees uprooted, with the peat still clinging to their roots. The only advantage that we had achieved was that the water was now so diminished that we could now wade the canoes across the river whenever the other side looked better. Here at last we could use a device I had thought of before we came. I don't know whether it is original with me, but it is quite effective where the water is deep enough and the current is not violent or irregular. In it, the towline is made fast to the midships thwart in the bight of a bowline large enough to slip from one side to the other so that the pull may be made from either side as desired according to the side of the river from which the tow is being made. A control line is then bent to the towline at a point abeam the towing ring at the bows when the tow line is stretched fore and aft. The control line is then weaved through a small pulley block tied to the ring and passed aft. By hauling taut on the control line the bows may be brought over to the towline side, and by paying out the bows may be allowed to swing out as the towline exerts a pull to turn the canoe away. With this system we have two men on the line ashore and one man in the canoe, seated amidships so that his weight does not affect the trim of the canoe. It worked very well that day where the going was good, and accounted for much of our speed the day after we left the canyon. It was a great help too where we had to follow a shoreline where trees and shrubs leaned more or less parallel to the water. Previously we had found these very difficult to pass along, but with the pulley control we were able to keep the canoe so far from shore that the towline tended to pass over the trees and their branches. But in fast water the control was not fast enough to be safe, and in shallow water the weight of the man in the boat was an added burden.

The ideal solution is for the man in the boat to jump out and wade alongside, guiding and pushing. A man alongside, determined, strong, and with his wits about him, can actually do more to get the canoe through tough places than two men working equally hard on the line ashore. The ideal would be to have a man alongside at all times, but he would have to be an exceptional man, for in comparison with the men ashore his footing is bad, being always unseen and often slippery, and he has to force his legs against a strong current often waist deep. Consequently he tires more quickly than the men ashore even when the going is good, and may not be able to keep the pace they can make. It is in such places that the pulley device is most useful; with it in use the control man can get in the canoe and rest up in easy places, and the whole party will move forward faster than if he had to wade alongside, holding the others back.

So much for the principle of the thing. In practice we tend to put old Bill in the canoe. And old Bill is a genius at doing the wrong thing. Torn between a desire not to be too big a burden on us and not to get his feet wet again, as soon as we came to a bad place he would drop the control line and grab a pole. The line would squeak through the block, the canoe would yaw, the pole would slip, and there would be old Bill broadside to the current again, and Jack and I barely able to hold him against the pull of the stream.

On August 23rd (Friday) we came to a mountain that we called Mount Symmetry, and under it the junction of two creeks with the Rat, which transform that river into a mere creek. But it would not be far that we would have to travel that creek. By our maps we were now within six miles, airline, from Loon Lake, and probably not over fifteen by river and canoe. And, for the time, our food supply problems were solved; the water here was clear enough for any self-respecting fish, and very shortly Bill's line brought us a welcome batch of Dolly Vardens. They were also a nuisance: Bill had to hold everything up while he photographed them in black and white, in colour, in still, and in motion pictures. And what most annoyed me was that right opposite us mountains and valleys rose in stunning majesty and in multitudinous variety, and the light, said Bill, was not good enough to take pictures of them. We'd never see them again; few people have ever seen them; none had seen them before us with as good a set of cameras as Bill had–and the light, he said, was not good enough. Instead he had to take pictures of fish identical to those he had been taking pictures of ever since he first owned a camera.

We did not get far that day. The place where we had camped the previous night remained in sight all day and we made our next camp possibly a mile and a half west of it. Yet we must have travelled ten miles by river, winding and twisting all through a wide valley. We saw a wolf that day, so thin and nearly hairless that it looked like a greyhound.

The next day I took over the canoe entirely, sending Bill up with Jack on the line. The river here was of the kind shown on the map as "braided", that is with numerous channels passing around gravel bars. Some of the channels were so small that the canoes had to be lifted and carried over them. Between riffles and rapids I rode in the big one, and on them jumped out and pushed or carried our two boats through. The braiding of the stream was a nuisance, both splitting the available supply of water and making it difficult to know how far we had come. Several times we had to walk ahead and make sure that some stream coming in from the side was merely a branch around an island, not another creek mingling with ours.

By August 24th (Saturday) we got through to the eastern shore of Loon Lake. Jack and I had threaded our way through niggerheads to the top of a small hill, from which we could see a series of small lakes to the west, with a big one at last, distant about three miles. We had a lovely view of the valley through which we had come and there saw a rainbow actually contained against the face of a hill. It was a pity we had no camera with us. The hill above the left bank of the stream was topped with unbroken lines of rock, 30 or 40 feet high, rising abruptly from the slope of the hills, and weathered sufficiently to suggest towers and crenellations. It seemed almost impossible to see them as natural formations, their appearance and their position being so suggestive of fortification walls built by man.

The going got better and better when we returned to the canoes. Paddling on we soon got to a small lake, where we had lunch by the side of a winter portage. Paddling again, we soon came to another "Y" in the river. The branch coming in from the left, slightly the larger, seemed likely to be the one shown on our map as the source of the Rat. The one on the right, which we followed, was unmapped. There was ample water in this creek for our canoes, and its banks were overgrown with stunted alder and willow, many of which had been eaten by beaver, and a few, we were glad to see, chopped down by axes. It did not prove very difficult to force our way through the bushes, and we came after a while to two old beaver dams, and one new one, and a small beaver lake. Shortly after this, with good paddling water, but several times stuck on the remains of yet older dams, we came to a comparably large lake with a good sound shore for a camp. We had travelled about six hours that day, going possibly twelve miles by water, and between two and three in a straight line. We ate the last of Bill's fish that night, and boiled the last of our rice. We had cooked the last of our rolled oats that morning.

Jack rather pointedly asked Bill that evening whether he had had the same companion twice in any of his previous trips. Bill, after delaying our start a full hour in the morning, had worked hard all day. He must have been tired. He did not answer.

On August 25th (Sunday) we got off to a fairly early start, got two miles of easy paddling where the stream ran almost still through a lake with banks overhung with willows and alder. We came then to another fork, with a small stream on the right, a larger one on the left, and an old camp, with a tin can turned bottom up on a long stake on the point between them. The stream on the right being obstructed by a beaver dam and overhung by a large spruce, we tried the stream on our left, but were soon stopped by a series of small rapids. Getting out on foot Jack and I explored, and eventually decided on the stream to the right. We had to unload the big canoe completely to get it over the dam we had seen there, and had to unload most of it again a while later to get it over another dam. This second dam was an active one, with fresh cuttings and a feed bed nearby. There seemed to be two beaver colonies here, one in this lake and one in the lake on whose shores we had camped the night before.

From the end of this small lake a well-worn portage crosses the tundra to Loon Lake. We packed one load over it; then Jack and Bill went back to prepare lunch, while I searched for a water connection between the two lakes. Jack and I both recalled Cliff Hagen's stating definitely that no portage was required here, and you could paddle directly to Loon Lake. Nevertheless, we had found no connecting waterway on our explorations that morning, and the creek we had followed seemed the most likely. In fact I did not expect to find any water connection. The portage we had found was sufficient argument against its existence. It was a well-worn portage, probably the main one used in winter, but also used in summer, for in one place four logs had been thrown across a streamlet to make better crossing. This stream was one of several running into the lake we had reached. I had counted four such so far, and between them they accounted for nearly all the water flowing out of the lake, leaving very little to make another stream from the lake.

So I started searching merely to make sure that I followed the shore of Loon Lake till I came to the hills on the north side of it, turned, and followed the shore the opposite way, till I came to a small creek leading into Loon Lake. It was heavily overgrown with stunted alder, and looked as if in dry weather it would go out of business altogether. I kept a little way back from it, avoiding the alders, but occasionally stepping through them, to make sure I was still in contact with an active stream, and not a dry channel. So for some distance: then I noticed that its current was running not from my left to my right, as before, but now from my right to my left. And I hadn't crossed it! I walked back a little way, peered through a small opening in the alder trees, and saw a small creek coming towards me, entering the valley I had been following, and there dividing, half to run one way, eventually, to the Mackenzie, and half the other way, eventually to the Yukon. So there was the water passage we had been seeking.

As a geographical feature it was interesting, but as a means of getting a canoe from one watershed to the other, it left much to be desired. If one laid an axe to the alders for a few days one might make a navigable stream of it, fit to drag a near empty canoe through it. The portage made by others was much simpler. We carried the dry goods over in one trip, returned to load the watertight container and some boxes of food in my small canoe, and worked all together to drag it through what we now called Two-Ocean creek, pushed and pulled my canoe back again, and finally lifted the large canoe, empty, upside down over my head and Jack's, Bill having gone ahead to look for a campsite.

So the next day, August 26th, we parted, my friends to go on, I to return to Aklavik. I was a little worried and sorry to leave them, sorry to let them go on without me, but very conscious of Jack's good sense and hard work all the way, and very forgiving of Bill's mannerisms and foibles. And at the sight of their canoe dwindling away down the valley of the Little Bell running off to the west I was suddenly eager myself to go exploring with them.

(I need not have worried about them. As I found out much later, a few miles after they left me they found a place where wolves had killed a moose and had left enough of it to feed them for the few days before they reached Fort Yukon. From there on they caught planes, and were home in Seattle again almost by the time I reached Aklavik.)

Chapter 7

Happy Birthday Back on the *Lady*

B ut that urge to explore was not to be. Two hundred miles to Aklavik, one thousand two hundred to Fort Nelson, six hundred to Edmonton–the sooner I started the sooner I'd be home again. By night time I was back on our previous camp on Loon Lake.

For all my long experience in canoes, I had never run rapids in them. When I was a youngster helping my brothers Frank and Jack in their trapline on the Hanging-Ice River we always portaged the few rapids we met. Now I had many miles ahead of me, to run alone, and, despite the rains we had met on the way up the water was much lower, so that my empty canoe sometimes touched bottom where we had dragged both canoes up afloat. I sat, or more often kneeled, in the stern end, with my blankets and other gear in the bow, and enjoyed every minute of it. Sometimes it was rough going, especially just past a rapids, still in it's swift water and running into contrary currents below it. Once I got dumped, but lost nothing, for my kit-bag and my sleeping robe were both attached to the painter, and within one or the other were my wallet, my watch, my gun, the diary I had been keeping, and what little food I had left. They bobbed merrily down stream while I got the canoe ashore and dumped it. And once, on one of the long straight runs a furious wind blowing straight up river turned my canoe completely around, and I went backwards down the next rapids, which I don't recommend to anyone, but caused me more amusement than danger.

On August 27, at about noon, I got to the place where I had made a little cache for myself, at the bottom of a series of riffles. I found everything in order, the little stock of warm clothing which I had thought I might need all dry and safe, and my dozen hardtack dry and good to eat, though a little mouldy at the bottom. I ate a couple of hardtack and went on, and continued munching them, with butter and a sardine paste which unaccountably had large fish eggs in it. The water had dropped and was much slower than when we had come up it, and the river also looked so much wider from my canoe than it had on the *Greenbelly* that I failed to recognize variable signs as I passed them, and so came, unexpecting, just when I had decided it must be miles ahead yet, to the mouth of the Rat.

My first view of the Husky showed a man in a green canoe, visiting a fish net. About 7:15 p. m. I met him, and by 8:30 I was away again, he richer by two dollars and I better off by a bellyful of boiled fish, 9 shotgun shells, some fine-cut tobacco and a packet of cigarette papers. He also told me that the reason we couldn't find Destruction City on our way up was that there is nothing left there to find. He also told me that it would take two hard days of paddling to reach Aklavik, and when I got into my canoe his last words to me were: "You should sit more in the middle; you'll upset if you sit at the end there." a remark which I, seated where I had been all through the rapids of the Rat, chose to ignore. This was the place which we had left on August 9th to arrive on Two-Ocean creek 17 days later, on August 26. Helped by the current, I had made it back in two days.

I paddled till dark that night, spread my mattress on the bottom of the canoe, squeezed my feet and knees in my robe on top of it, stretched out, and would have slept comfortably while drifting down the Husky except that there were just enough mosquitoes to wake me now and again. I rigged a sort of sail to help the current after I got up, and about 4 p.m. came upon a fishnet in an eddy, helped myself to a fish—a Dolly Varden, and so much for Bill and his self-respecting fish and muddy water. Immediately around the point was a tent, a fish stage, and an Indian who came out with his gun when his dogs barked. I told him about the fish and said I would not have taken it without asking him if I had known he was so close, and how much did he want for it? He didn't want anything, and said take another if I wanted it, and just before I pulled away he asked "Is there anything else I could do for you?" I asked him how long it would take to reach

Aklavik from there. "Seven hours" he said, and it didn't occur to me till much later that he meant it would take him that long with use of his kicker in his canoe.

So I went on, at first intent on getting to Aklavik in time for a piece of pie at Cliff's before he closed for midnight, then equally intent on getting there in time for breakfast before it went off at ten, then on getting there in time for dinner at noon; and finally disgusted with the non-appearance of the Peel, I laid down and would have gone to sleep except for the mosquitoes, which did not seem to mind the cold as much as I. I paddled then through such dark that I could barely see the shores, until the river turned back towards the mountains, the mosquitoes disappeared, and I went to bed and slept till morning, drifting.

When I woke next the sun was shining, the mosquitoes were out again, I was just drifting out of the Husky into the Peel, and it was my thirty-ninth birthday. I was in Aklavik and aboard the Lady Greenbelly by 11. I cleaned up and then had a piece of pie at the lunch counter, had two bowls of soup for dinner, two helpings of main course, six pieces of pie, then had another piece of pie at the lunch counter, sent wires off to Jack's mother and to Barbara, had a piece of pie, repaired my canoe where I had split the end board a trifle, had a piece of pie, and then had supper with Bell and Ruth.

Then I settled in the *Lady Greenbelly* and for what I think was the first time, felt at home in her. She was my boat, and I had built a cabin on her, had my own comfortable bed in her, my own cooking arrangements, places to hang my clothes, my tools, my letters, my personal belongings. She was *my* boat, had given me trouble, would undoubtedly give me more trouble (had even given Albert trouble on his trip back to Aklavik from where he had left us, running out of gas, forcing him to walk the last few miles to get some more.) Much of the trouble she had given me was of my own making, and in return she had given me two joys that I would never have known without her: Mike Krutko on my way down river with her, and Jack Havens in Aklavik and Tuk-Tuk and now somewhere nearing home on the other side of Two-Ocean Creek. I would part with *Lady Greenbelly* sometime in some happy future, but the memory of those two men would stay with me, and be a model for me, each in his own way, for the rest of my life. And old Bill, too, now that I did not have to put up with his mannerisms and pretensions, I could almost admire his courage and hope that at his age I would not be harder to put up with than I had found him.

I rejoiced a while in my memories, then turned to face a problem: How on earth was I going to get the said *Lady Greenbelly* back south to Fort Nelson before winter froze up the rivers she must travel in?

Chapter 8

The *Lady* Back at Aklavik

Life got very complicated for me almost as soon as I got back into Aklavik. The first thing Macauley said to me was "Now, there's luck for you! Here the *Slave* is due in tomorrow and I was just wondering who I could get to check Pfeffer's freight off her, and here Conibear arrives." Mac had been a very good friend of mine all that summer, and I couldn't let him down. And while waiting I had a chance to pull the stern of the *Lady Greenbelly* out and have another go at her rudders and propellor. With some help from Bell on welding parts of the rudder harness, some advice from nearly everyone who came by while I was working the propellor over, and further help from Bell in using the *Aurora* to pull the *Lady* back into the water again, that effort substantially increased her speed and ease of handling.

Meantime I chanced to get in touch with Poole Field, an old friend of our family, now settled in Aklavik, whom I had promised to visit if ever I got free in the evening. It chanced that when I was free he had two other old-timers visiting him, and they had a bottle, and he was soon telling them (and me) a story that an old rediscovered friend had told him about another man, now dead, who had found rich gold in what Poole thought was the Canoe River. In fact the other two knew the story as well as Poole and most of the evening was passed in trying to convince him that it was not the Canoe but the next one west, known either as the Firth or the Herschel Island River. Further, the man who told the story of gold being found in one of those rivers running into the North Sea west of the Mackenzie delta was a man called Blake. He had been a trader for the Hudson's Bay on Herschel Island; an Eskimo one day had brought him a sample of gold as a curiosity; Blake has asked him to take him to the place where it could be found; the Eskimo, Blake, and Blake's son, then about age thirteen, had gone together; they carried a little grub in their packs, but could not stay more than a few days; but in those few days Blake panned enough gold nearly to fill an Eno's Fruit Salt bottle. Blake always meant to go back, but his wife was ill; then he was ill; then he died. His son had told Poole. Poole thought the *Lady Greenbelly* would be ideal for getting out to the river and running up it a short distance, to supply prospectors with somewhere to sleep and sufficient supply of provisions. So, would I go with him, to stake and pan? When? This fall, or when I came back next spring? But one of Poole's friends interjected again that it wasn't the Canoe River, it was the Firth River. Moreover, he said, Macauley had been there and would know which river it was on. So MacAuley was sent for, and came. "Sure" he said, "he'd been there; he knew the country well, had gone with a party, and all was true about the gold; but the party as a whole were very lousy, and he didn't like being lousy, and had simply walked out on them, cutting his rights down to a single large nugget which he wanted for a stickpin, which he never got because of Blake's dying; and it took him three months to boil the lice out of his shirts and bedding after he got back". He'd always meant to go back, knew the very place where he would start working, had even picked the spot where he would shoot the wild goat that would feed him long enough to make a fortune there.

More people, with more bottles, then dropped in, and I was lucky to get back to sleep by midnight. I was tempted to go prospecting with Poole, but it seemed too late in the year to go now. Surely it would be better to go in the spring, after bringing down a load of goods for someone in Aklavik.

The next day the *Slave* came in and kept me busy checking freight for Macauley. There was also freight for me—a plywood canoe and a kicker. Both should have been here on the first boat from Fort Smith. No letter had come from Northwest Industries, {the company that had been making plywood bombers during the War}. So I didn't know whether it was a gift charged to publicity, or whether I would eventually have to pay for it. Anyway I was glad to have the kicker, in case I shouldn't be able to get the *Lady* beyond the junction of the Fort Nelson and the Liard this fall. I could pull her out somewhere there and travel the rest of the way with canoe and kicker.

When I got the Macauley's freight off that evening I looked for a helper to accompany me in the *Lady*, and found an excellent one. He was a man whom our party in Fort Nelson that spring had got to know so often that he became "the man who eats with us". He was now in Aklavik, working for a company building boats for sale in the delta. He heard I was thinking of going back to Fort Nelson, and said he'd like to come with me, if he could get a release from his employers. His name was Charley Koska and he would be the ideal mate for me on the venture, a most agreeable soul, a good worker, experienced in travel on the Slave, the Liard, and the Fort Nelson. I went to see his employers that same day, and before I mentioned his name I was asked if I could take him back with me.

So we started on September 6th, reached Arctic Red River that night, Thunder River the following night. The propellor and the rudders worked better than I had dared to hope but the engine gave us a problem, running too hot, at 202 degrees. At Good Hope on the tenth the Signals Sergeant took a look at it and told me not to worry about overheating as long as there was water going through. He seemed certain that the thermometer must be "on the bum"–with which I was happy to agree. He said there was a possibility that the Roman Catholic Mission might have a suitable left hand propellor. So to the Mission I went, found no propeller but did find Father Robin, who, on hearing my name almost burst into tears. He explained that he had come into the North thirty-four years ago, the same year as Mother with her five children. He remembered our names: Frank, Dolly, Jack, Mabel, and was I really the little fellow known as "Kinnet"? He remembered seeing us at Grande Rapids ("Rapides" he called them, with accent on the last syllable but pronounced the first syllable as we do.) But he could not recall the name of the little side-wheel steamer that refused to work there. "Saint Joseph" or "Sainte Therese"–he could not remember which, and I did not tell him that in the history of the Conibear family she was still referred to as the "Pollywog".

At that point we were interrupted by a lay brother who came in and spoke something in French. Father Robin listened a while, then looked at me and said; "We have a problem, and if you are like your father perhaps you can help us with it. Come this way, please." In a few minutes we were standing beside an almost new, shiny, yellow power plough and Father Robin was explaining to me that its share refused to stay up when wanted up: it seemed determined to plow at all times. He explained what they had done and what they proposed to do. It just happened that in utter indifference to ploughs and how they operate, I chanced to see what was wrong with that one. The share should be kept in position by means of a ratchet fitting into notches on a semi-circular strut, and somewhere, somehow that strut had got bent, and the ratchet did not connect in the "up" position. I advised that they put a blow-torch to the strut and try to hammer it straight again. The lay brother seemed to understand, and rushed off to try it, and Father Robin and I walked outside and for the first time he saw the boat that had brought me here.

"What do your call it?" he asked.

"The *Lady Greenbelly*".

Perhaps it was only the first part of my answer that he heard. He said "I like that. I suppose if you don't feel that you can use a saint's name 'Lady' does something the same." He paused and looked around "Are you going up the Rampart rapids in *that*?"

"I hope so," I said.

"If you find you can't make it come back here and we'll be happy to put you up till a plane comes. And as for your boat, the Mission used to have a small sidewheeler here, and kept it in the winter a little way up the Hare Indian River. I think the capstans are still there. If not, we could get the tractor we use in our gardens to pull the *Lady* out."

We walked back to the Mission then, after a brief inspection of the marvelous art work done in the church by some priest or brother many years ago, we were met by the lay brother triumphantly waving from the power-plough. So we said "goodbye."

"Your father was a good man." He remarked. "When he came down here as engineer on ships he used often to look in on us and to try to repair anything wrong with our machinery. He had a sense of humour too. That old sidewheeler we had here, you know what he called her?"

"I'd hate to tell you," I said, "but yes, he was the finest man I've ever known."

"And the North was different then," said Father Robin. "People used to help each other then–Catholics, Protestants, Indian, White men–everyone."

"People still do," I insisted. "You've just proved it."

I looked up then, and saw that two tears had formed in his eyes, and were slowly rolling down and falling on his beard. There he had an advantage over me: he could reach up with his clerical robe and wipe them cleanly away. Mine stayed where they fell.

Chapter 9

The *Lady* at the Ramparts

So we got away, Charley and the *Lady Greenbelly* and I and our overheating engine on September 11th. We came through the Ramparts, the towering cliffs on each side of the river a permanent feature of the country, beloved of camera packing tourists. It was a still bright evening, with the sun aft and to starboard, and I found them lovely. I noticed five caves in the right wall, and in several places an overhang of perhaps ten feet at the very top. A thin line of earth, bearing stunted trees, rested on top of the rocks; and in the crevices a few shrubs and moss grew; but generally the face was bare, a brownish grey of sharp rectangular edges. I enjoyed it that night as I never had before. I suppose that when I had come through them in the summer of 1928 as a fireman on the *Distributor* I had always been off watch or too busy keeping up steam to fully enjoy them. True, I'd seen them as we came through in the *Lady Greenbelly* that spring, but my interest then had been entirely concentrated on recovering what we could out of what we had lost when flooded out at Norman Wells.

About three miles above these universally famous Ramparts of the Mackenzie River lie the locally infamous Ramparts Rapids. The Rapids are a temporary feature only, hated by the riverboat captains who happen to find themselves below them in the fall of the year.

A three mile long ledge of limestone stretching fair across the river, straight as a ruler all the way, but not quite level on top, is the cause of the Rapids. In the summer the whole ledge is covered by water, and boats of all kinds pass freely across it, running upstream or down. When the water-level drops in the autumn, however, the picture is quite different. Two miles of acre-large flat islands stretching in a chain from the left bank, a half-mile of tumbling cascade reaching out towards the islands from the right bank, and between the cascade and the islands a long chute of smoothly, swiftly racing water–that is the Ramparts Rapids any time after the end of August.

The only navigable channel at that time of the year is through the chute, fairly close to the outermost of the chain of islands–a long flat monster known anywhere on the river, and identified without further description, simply as "the Rock". This channel is not navigable in the sense that the Atlantic is navigable by the *Queen Elizabeth*. I doubt whether there is a boat on the Mackenzie capable of climbing the chute on its own power once the water-level has dropped.

Here was the greatest challenges of all I had that summer. If I could somehow get the *Lady* on the other side of these rapids I had at least a possibility of getting her up to Fort Nelson, ready to go to work next spring. If I couldn't, there was nothing for it but to turn back to Good Hope and lay her up there as Father Robin had suggested, or to Aklavik and try to sell her for whatever I could get, hoping it would be enough to buy me a flight back to Edmonton–if, indeed any more flights would be scheduled before freeze-up.

For this reason, I was much worried lest the *Peel River* might have passed through them before we got there. The skipper, Lunky Thorvaltsen, an old friend of mine, had promised to try to tow us through them, and she had passed us while we were stuck on a sandbar the previous night. However, we made it, reached the rapids on September 12th, found the *Peel* still there, and tied up inside her barges.

The *S.S. Peel River,* ancient stern-wheeler though she is, is about the fastest of all the stern-wheelers on the river, and even Lunky says she can't climb the chute. He tried it once. He tried it, in fact, only one day before Charley and the *Lady Greenbelly* and I groaned our way through the Ramparts and discovered with pleasure that Lunky was still on the same side of the Rapids as we were.

"Two men and a boy sitting on the safety valve" he told me that same day, "and both firemen just pouring wood into the boiler, I

67

reckon she was making anyway fifteen knots. How fast you reckon the water comes down the chute, Ken?"

"I'm no judge" I said, but when he insisted that I make a guess, I hazarded "fifteen knots, maybe."

Lunky shook his great Nordic head. "Thirteen mebbe, fourteen mebbe. I don't know."

"So you made it, Lunky?"

"No. I make it right up to the top all right, right over the hump and into level water beyond. Then—well, you can guess what happened then. The bow dropped, the stern lifted, the wheel came out, we slid back. Then we went forward again, over the hump again. Then the bow dropped again. Then we slid back again. Hell! a fellow could keep that up till the Indians paid their debts."

"Go easy, Lunky" I said. "Blue moons are safer."

He laughed his great Valkyrian laugh.

"Damn foolishness anyway, Ken. I still had my three barges tied up in this cove here. Damn waste of company firewood. Four cords of the very best that bit of fun cost us, and even if I had made the rapids with the steamer alone I knew damn well she'd never push the barges up the chute, even one at a time."

I had been wondering about that myself. Lunky had always seemed to me one of the most sensible men I knew. I could imagine myself playing about in the rapids for the sheer folly of it, but not Lunky. I waited for his explanation.

"I guess I'm as bad as the rest of the damn fools on this hooker" he said. "I did it just to show off to that girl."

He gave the simpering little laugh men will when they thus accuse themselves—even modern Vikings like Lunky. I knew at once what girl he referred to, and I lost interest rapidly. In the few hours since I had tied up beside the *Peel* I had already heard all I wanted of the exotic passenger she carried.

"What's the plan now?" I asked.

"Ain't got any for today" he said. "*Slave* went up day before yesterday, found that hunk of cable you fellows left on shore way back in nineteen twenty eight, used it, left me a note, said don't trust it, it just got 'em over the hump when it busted. Day after tomorrow the Rapids Boat will be down—bringing a ninety horse winch and four spools of three-quarter cable. They'll make one end fast to the deadman two miles up the shore, then float down, reeling it out

68

behind them. We'll pull as soon as they enter the rapids, and be waiting for them when they get through. We'll take the winch aboard the steel barge–there's lots of room to work on her–lash barge 106 on her starboard, 108 on her port, you behind 106, me behind the steel barge, Rapids Boat behind 108, all engines going. You'll have a snug lie there, Ken."

This is what I had been waiting to hear. Without help I stood no chance of ever getting up those rapids.

"It's good of you, Lunky, mighty good of you" I said.

"Forget it" he answered at once. "In this country you never know–you may be able to do as much for me sometime."

That was good for a laugh anywhere from Aklavik to Fort Simpson, of course; but I chose to take it seriously.

"If ever I can, I will," I promised.

That ended the conversation. Lunky's lady passenger, more heavily painted than I remember seeing any other white woman in the North, chose this moment to appear on the *Peel*'s bowdeck below us, surrounded by a large group of admiring males. Lunky leaned over the rail to look down at the gathering. I made my way aft to the many problems that awaited me on my own small boat.

I suppose it was largely the admiration she elicited from the other men around that at first gave me the wrong impression of Linda Driver–if it was a wrong impression at that time. Some rich old buzzard's spoilt daughter down to take a quick look at the country, to get a vicarious thrill of some kind out of the life other people live in it, to talk and act later in her own country as if she knew all there was to know about this one–such I gathered she was, and such I had seen quite enough of in my own North already. I didn't hold her money against her, of course, and hope I no longer have any prejudices about what a woman may choose to put on her face; but it did seem to me that her kind of charm was out of place in that situation, and that we would all be better off without her presence, even though none of the other men seemed to think so.

She was used to getting her own way. I suppose it was quite a shock to her when she heard the reception I gave to the proposition she put to me on my second day of waiting below the Rapids. She entered my pilot-house door as if she owned it, rested her feet on my engine room steps, cupped her chin in her hands, and watched me brood over my engine.

"I flew from Fairbanks to Tuktoyaktuk" she began. She had a pleasant voice; she was the only woman I've ever known who could pronounce "Tuktoyaktuk" correctly without sounding as if she had just laid an egg. "I wanted to see what the country looked like, and when I heard that the *Peel* was coming back up the Mackenzie and I could get passage on her, I was delighted."

Perhaps I did hold her money against her, after all. I remember wondering what she had done with her return ticket to Fairbanks. It would represent more than all the money I hoped to make, and save, this trip with my boat. I said nothing.

"It's been nice on the *Peel*" she went on after a while. "It was quite thrilling at first; but I feel now that I've already had all the thrills it is going to give me. You—you don't see much of the real life of the country on a boat like her. I realised that when I saw you and Charley pull in beside us yesterday."

She looked about her at the little cabin I had built over the engine of my scow, at the greasy tools hanging on the walls, the boxes nailed up for food-cupboards, the tin dishes on their crazy shelves.

"Where do you cook your meals?" she asked.

"We don't" I said.

"I hear you're going through to Fort Nelson on the Alaska highway."

"That's the idea" I said, and I picked up a screwdriver and started to fiddle about with the commutator in what might have passed among the Dog-Rib Indians as a knowledgeable way.

"I wonder—could you take me with you?"

I can't be so stupid as I seem at times. I had seen this coming, and had my answer ready.

"No" I said.

"No? Just like that?"

"No."

"I'd pay the same fare as on the *Peel*—more if you wish."

I should have stuck to plain "No" and saved myself much trouble. The reason I didn't, I suppose, was that there was a very earnest little face looking at me from under the paint and powder.

"I've no license, Linda. I'm not allowed to take passengers."

"Good. That's what I want, to work my way, to be part of your crew, to help. And I could buy your gasoline and food supplies.

70

That's the way they get around that regulation in this country, isn't it?"

It was, and I had been looking for someone to do that ever since I left Aklavik–but not Linda Driver.

"No," I said.

"Why not, Ken?"

Blue eyes she had, and quite as deep as if her old man didn't own two banks and a department store in New York. I stuck the screwdriver in a deck-crack, and stood up before her.

"It's a tough trip in this outfit" I said, "tough for a man, impossible for a woman. Any woman."

That was the worst mistake yet. She got out a packet of cigarettes, had me light two, and settled down for a nice long talk.

"Give me all the reasons" she said.

"First: the motor–it overheats" I answered. "Second: the shaft–it's bent. Third: the prop–it's way out of wang. We'll be lucky if we make Simpson without trouble from all three. Fourth: the boat–it's narrow and wall-sided–"

I stopped. She had got down off the steps and was bending over my engine.

"I used to work on a motor like that when I was in the Spars" she said. "A V-8 marine. Some people don't like them. I do. Give me the symptoms. What was the gauge reading when you came in yesterday?"

"Two-twenty" I said.

"Did you ever try putting the gauge on the other bank?"

I blinked. I had never thought of that.

"If one side is blocked" she said, "it will run too hot, and the other side will get too much water and run too cold. It will get all the water, in fact, and hardly heat it up at all. What was the water like when it came out of the engine?"

"We used to make cocoa from it and drink it as soon as it was drawn" I said.

"She shuddered. "Awful stuff, I'll bet. That's the trouble then. I'll have the eleven sixty-fourth box-end please."

Two hours later we went out for a trial run. Linda remained in the engine room, shifting gears for me, checking temperature, checking plugs, while I ploughed the *Lady* round and round in the strong water below the rapids.

71

"Running at one sixty constant, Captain" she reported finally, saluting quite expertly, and blinking at me a set of eye-lashes long as muskrat whiskers.

Perhaps someone else can explain why I turned the boat's nose toward the rapids as the girl came and stood beside me at the tiller.

"I never got my hands on a boat's wheel all through the war" she said.

Neither had I. I let her take it.

She drove us into the heavy stuff at the bottom of the chute without flinching, bore down on the throttle as far as it would go, forced us right through that raging maelstrom of eight foot waves and giant swirling eddies. In the calmer and faster water of the chute proper I took over. We climbed then till the big hole in the water at the upper tip of the Rock yawned not ten feet off our starboard bow. There we hung, unable to make any further headway, a bedlam of mechanical noises in a bedlam of watery ones.

Not till we were nearly back to the *Peel* did I think of the harm I might have done my boat in that venture. All the way from Aklavik Charley and I, mindful of the *Lady*'s crooked shaft, had never opened the throttle wide. I remembered Lunky's words then: "I guess I'm as bad as the rest of the damn fools, Ken. I just did it to show off to the girl."

It was an unlucky time for Linda to put her proposition to me again, and an unfortunate way she chose to put it:

"Well, Ken Conibear?"

"No." It was as flat a "no" as ever at first, but the disappointment in her eyes made me quickly amend it.

"I'm sorry, Linda" I said.

I meant that.

The lower tip of the Rock showed even with my pilot-house door. This was the spot where I had taken the wheel from Linda the day before. The water between me and the Rock poured in a smooth sluice a hundred feet wide, its surface a sliding velvet on which slow eddies rolled. It seemed that the water was still, the Rock animate, a great grey flat-backed creature powerfully swimming.

On the other side, the *Peel* leaked steam at every crack. Windows, port-holes, great freight-doors, all exuded creeping wraiths that took sudden wings as the outdoor winds caught them. Her safety-valve screamed continually, her boiler door never ceased its banging open and shut.

The after-wave of the barge 106 ahead of me was a static curve upon the water, continually sliding away astern, continually shouldering onward, yet forever fixed in its relation to me. Where it first rose it was a raging wall of angry voice, clamouring to sweep over me and all I had, resistless. Continually I advanced upon it, wall and voice, continually it receded in front of me.

The wake rising from under the barge was a bubble-streaked hollow curving upward. Part broken by my bows, conflicting in heard but unseen violence with the bow-wave of the *Peel*, reforming, it built another mound upon the water, churning over at right angles to my gunnel–a roaring lion drawn backward by an invisible leash, ten feet in front of me. Broken parts of it, struggling out from under the *Lady*'s flat bottom, occasionally tore the smooth surface apart with great erupting bubbles. They only, rising always in different places, momently altered the water-pattern about me.

Half hypnotized, I turned my eyes away, looked into my small engine room. Oil-covered water rocked gently in the well under the glimmering shaft. I went down the three steps, leaned over the pulsating engine, wobbled my hand-pump up and down til oil and air came up with the plunger.

When I returned to my pilot-house we had stopped our slow movement up the chute. Charley came aboard off 106, walked aft toward me along the catwalk, balancing himself with out-stretched arms. He sang his usual song.

"'Now Esau was a hairy man, Of wild and woolly make; His pa left half his farm to him, and half to brother Jake'. Take a spell, Ken. Get off and look around. It'll be anyways a quarter hour before we get mov'n again."

"What's happened, Charley?"

He warbled on as I asked my question.

"'But Esau coming home one day, Was feeling kind of queer'. Damn slack of the cable came in faster than they could reel it up."

"That's odd" I said. "They're not short-handed, with all those passengers helping."

"Short-handed–hell! That was the trouble, I guess. Too many of them. Fall'n all over each other. And that girl–"

"Linda Driver? Was she helping too?"

"I guess so. Watch'n mebbe, help'n mebbe. And everybody scairt o hurt'n her with the damn stuff. Anyways the mate kicked her off the barge and told her not to come back till we're over the rapids."

I liked Charley. Besides myself, he seemed to be the only man around with a sensible attitude toward the girl. He laughed now. I laughed too.

He went on with his song.

"'So he sold his half to Jacob for a sandwich and a beer'. Nice day, ain't it, Ken?"

Half an hour later we were stopped again. Charley came aboard again.

"'Now Joseph was a flashy guy, A zoot-suit man was he'. It'll be anyways a half-hour this time, Ken.

"What's happened, Charley?"

"'A razzle-dazzle coat he wore, Despite his familee'. Damn steam dropped. Clear down to eighty pound. Sand-clinkers plugged the boiler-screen."

I turned to look at the steamer's great red wheel visible through my after-window. It was turning, but slowly, slowly, moved only by the water that streamed against its blades.

"Yeah" said Charley. "The line's all that's holding us now, Ken. Lunky says if it breaks he'll shoot Thad."

"My God! Have you been up there?"

"Yeah, sure. Me, I think it's going to break."

I sent Charley back to the barge in a hurry, with instructions to stand by with the hatchet, ready to cut my lines in three strokes if I gave him the signal. I did not like the situation at all. Neither, I know, did Lunky. And as for Thaddeus Macdonald, the *Peel*'s chief engineer, he must have steam up inside him equal to the best his boiler had ever produced. Even if the cable held, he'd lose his job over this, if Lunky logged it as he might.

The line held. Half an hour we hung there, impotent in the fury around us, while men watched the boiler-gauge creep gradually upwards. Then steam was gently let into the cylinders once more, blown out in great hissing clouds through the release ports aft. It was given a full head then, sent shouting up the stack in a triumphant "chough-chough-chough-chuff!" We began to crawl slowly forward again.

I was still thinking about Thad. It wasn't entirely Thad's fault that the steam had dropped. I could remember hearing his objecting to burning driftwood in the boiler while waiting for the Rapids Boat, Lunky's answering that they were running short of good fuel and must save what they had for the trial ahead. So in a way it was Lunky's fault: he should have seen that enough was taken on at the last wood-pile. It was odd that he had not.

Then suddenly I remembered:–"Four cords we burnt on that bit of fun, Ken... just to show off to that girl."

I reached around to pat myself on the back then.

"No... No, I'm sorry Linda, I can't." It was a mighty good word to have the use of, that "No." Half of mankind's wisdom lay in that one syllable.

We were stopped again, near the head of the Rock now. There was a pair of rounded projections on the top of the Rock which reminded me of a turtle and its half-withdrawn head. We had been approaching it for time unknown, were abreast of it at last. On the farther shore was a grey gash in the bank fit to make a similarly conspicuous marker. Inch by inch Turtle and Gash had crept to alignment, Turtle approaching me slowly, Gash marching sedately under the horizon, remote, unperturbed, aloof to the turmoil here. So they came at last one behind the other, like rear and foresights in a gun held wrong end to, Turtle first, then Gash. And in that position they stayed.

Yet we were not motionless. Turtle continually grew smaller before my eyes. For some reason Lunky was swinging us far to the other side of the channel, away from the Rock.

Then suddenly he started to swing us back again. The foot-wide gap between his boat and mine closed abruptly. I felt a little shock, a gently meeting of wood and wood it seemed. The *Peel*'s catwalk and the overhang of my engine room rode at about the same height. To prevent chafing, an old truck tire had been hung between them, suspended on a rope from a stanchion of the steamer's saloon deck. The rope parted suddenly, all in the space of a second, as if there were no more strength in it than in gossamer.

The *Lady* took the shock and lurched away from her larger mate, opening the gap momentarily. At once it closed again, and the heavy truck tire, released one moment, pinched on its edge the next, flew

75

suddenly ten feet in the air, passed over my pilot-house, and instantly disappeared in the water astern.

The *Lady* lurched again, leaned far over to starboard till the water was a hissing violence not two inches below my gunnel, then slowly righted. Inch by inch the *Peel's* catwalk crept up the outside wall of my engine room, ploughed unhesitatingly through the thin trimming at its top, and then, pushing roof-canvas and its affixing nails before it, slipped quickly over the roof till it jarred to a stop against the higher side of my pilot-house.

We continued to swing across-stream towards the Rock. A wall of water grew slowly against my starboard side. It was a mere ripple pushed in front of us at first, but gradually crept further up the side as the full force of the chute pressed more directly against it. Ten feet forward of my position, where the roaring line still reared its foaming crest, splashes of water began to trickle inboard.

I was quite alone. Charley had deserted his post on the barge. I could see no one against the railing above me, no one on the *Peel's* bow close alongside.

It was useless to think of pumping by hand. I could never hope to keep up with that creeping flood already risen to the shaft of my engine. The end would come quickly: the *Lady* would sink deeper as water accumulated within her; suddenly the engine-roof would slip free; suddenly the starboard side would be borne down by the weight of current pressing against it. Suddenly, and soon, an angry wall of water would burst through my pilot-house door.

Inevitably that door, the one legal exit from both engine-room and pilot-house, was on the wrong side for my safety. The mere addition of my weight as I went through the door and rounded my engine-room would push the starboard gunnel down another inch.

There remained my pilot-house windows. I had my head and shoulders out before I saw Linda. She came on the run from some-where forward, leapt over the maze of cables on the *Peel's* bow, and leaned out toward me.

"Linda, see Lunky, quick. Tell him I'm sinking. Ask him to go over on the other tack, quick!"

"The cable's caught on a rock in the bottom, Ken. They're doing this to free it, they hope."

"Linda! Please! Quick!"

She went, slowly at first, then racing up the gangway steps as my words came home to her.

The Turtle was growing small again, and I was down in my engine room, pumping furiously, when she returned. I heard her rapping on the roof over my head.

"Will you get Charley, Linda? As soon as Lunky is as far over as he can get, I want Charley to cut me loose."

Her face went white under its artificial colouring.

"No" she said.

"Yes" I said. "I'll be all right. The bow will drop when she's free of the tow, the stern come up. She'll float high then."

"No" she screamed.

"Yes" I shouted.

I was pumping again when she came back. The roof had slipped out from under the *Peel*'s catwalk, and the *Lady* was rocking freely, sloshing her bilge-water from side to side.

Linda was alone.

"Linda, where's Charley?"

She had something to say to me, and stepped down onto my port gunnel to make her way closer to my ear, down into the gap between the two boats. My engine-room roof was level with her stomach, the *Peel*'s catwalk even against the small of her back–and as I watched I saw the two of them gently swinging towards each other, gently, just as they had when they had pinched the tire and flung it ten feet in the air.

"Look out!" I shrieked.

I could have saved her quite easily. All I had to do was to swing my wheel over, to jam my rudders to port. I never thought of that. I shot out of my one door, rounded my engine-room, pushed myself into the gap between the two boats, pressed with hands and elbows against the great white wall in front of me.

Some vast eddy in the waters saved us both, or perhaps some unnoticed trifling turn on Lunky's wheel. He could not see us from where he was. Anyway, the pressure relaxed, and Linda scrambled up on my roof.

The *Lady* heeled violently from side to side, top-heavy and maddened by the water within her. Linda's body slipped on the engine-room roof. She seized the pilot-house window framing, held on with white fingers. I shouted to her to let go and back off. She only clung tighter. I tried to grasp her ankles, to pull her off. I could not reach them. I shouted again. It was all useless. I doubt whether she heard me.

I squirmed hurriedly along the starboard gunnel. The *Lady* heeled violently under my weight. A six inch wave followed me through the pilot-house door. I rushed to port, seized the girl's hands, and drew her in through the window.

"Out that door and back on the Peel. Quick!"

She clung to me.

"Hurry, Linda! She's going down!"

There could be no doubt of it now. The next wave would be continuous, filling the boat. Rope or bollard would give then, and the *Lady* would drift astern, her gunnels awash, her engine dead.

"Hurry!" I cried again.

She wouldn't budge. She wouldn't move from me. She lifted her mouth close to my ear.

"They're bringing a pump" she said.

Even as she spoke Charley and one of the deck-hands burst through the rear door of the centre barge, lugging a portable two-lunger between them. They set it on the *Peel*'s deck, started it with one pull of the cord (I've never seen that happen before), and swung the three-inch intake hose into the gap between the boats.

I've never had much use for two-lungers of any kind, but I must admit that that one was a miracle of efficiency and good-will. I hadn't any more than nipped down into my engine-room and drawn the hose through the port-hole before I felt the water shrinking away about my legs. My part in the "Men Against the River" sequence from then on consisted of a desperate battle with the dozen loaves of bread I had lifted from the *Peel*'s galley. The last lurch had brought them all tumbling down into my bilge-water. They at once began a circling rush towards the pump's intake, blocked it, disintegrated, crumbled to pieces in my clutching hands. The pump made rude noises at me then, grabbed at my fingers, and released them only to take a limpet hold on the slack of my trousers.

Lunky was idly gazing at his charts of the river south of the Ramparts when I went up to his pilot-house to see him.

"Thanks for sending that pump, Lunky. If it hadn't been for that–"

A great Norse blankness spread over his features.

78

"What pump, Ken?"

I went down to see Charley, found him loading our valuables on the *Lady* again.

"Good thing you thought of that pump, Charley. It saved us."

His face looked more like an owl's than ever.

"Wasn't my idee, Ken. I seen a fellow struggling with it and since Linda had told me to go the same way, I helped him."

I went to see the mate, found him directing the operation of reeling in the slack cable, a mile and a half still to go.

"Thanks for sending the pump, Bill. If it hadn't been–"

Bill's face never showed any emotion. He left that entirely to his tongue.

"So that's where the damn thing got to!" he exclaimed. "Now, how the hell did it get there?"

I went to see Lunky again.

"That was a damn close-run thing" he said. "Have a drink. First the cable snarls about the barge. You heard how that happened, didya, Ken?"

"Yes" I said.

"Then the steam drops–"

"And we both know the reason for that, you and I, the ultimate reason" I interrupted. I was fond of Thad.

Lunky slowly nodded his great blond head.

"Yes" he agreed.

"She wants to leave you and go the rest of the way with me" I said. "I don't want to take her. I haven't said I would. How would you feel if I did?"

He thought it over a long time.

"You remember when we were talking about my helping you up the rapids the day you pulled in, and you promised you'd do as much for me if you ever got the chance?" he asked slowly at last. "Well, I'm thinking I might call the whole business square if you took that blasted female to hell off my boat."

I sighed.

"That's what I was afraid you'd say, Lunky. But I'm not promising yet."

"I quite understand" he said.

I went to see Linda then.

"About that pump–" I began, but she wasn't answering anybody's questions just at that moment. She was asking them.

"Well, Ken Conibear?"

Some day I hope she'll write her own version of this story and let me read it. I still can't figure out for myself just why I answered as I did then.

"Yes, Linda" I said. So much for mankind's 'word of wisdom'!

Chapter 10

The Lady Becomes a Lady

Linda Driver's initiation into the hard realities of life aboard the *Lady Greenbelly* began when we hit a gravel bar in the shallows below Sans Sault Rapids. We struck hard, running at our normal half-throttle, bounced, ploughed forward our full fifty-foot length, then struck again. Aft in the pilot-house, Charley changed gears, revved up, revved down, ground his rudders to starboard, ground his rudders to port, swore humorously, swore long-sufferingly, swore savagely–all without effect. He shut off the engine and tugged at the sounding pole beside the door.

"Sounds bad, Linda" I said. "I'd better go help him."

Five minutes later Charley and I went overside together. That five minutes was spent by us in prying about fruitlessly with our pushing poles, by Linda in changing from skirt and blouse to slacks and sweater. She had said that she wanted to be a help to us in any troubles we met: she now dressed accordingly and emerged from under the canvas shelter burning to get out and prove how useful she could be. What she saw when she first came into the open was about five square miles of grey Mackenzie River sliding swiftly by. What she heard was a big splash forward, followed by much grunting and wheezing under the *Lady*'s high bow.

I suppose her reaction was quite natural. She let out a little shriek, grabbed our one and only life-buoy from its holder on the engine room roof, and heaved it at us. For so frail a creature, she had a strong arm and a remarkably good aim. The buoy planked fair between us, and splashed our faces liberally. We both bent hurriedly to seize it before the current could carry it off, both got a bump on the head from the other fellow's. Charley's fingers were the first to touch it. He heaved it back aboard.

Linda and the returning life-buoy reached the bow-deck at the same time. Startled, she picked it up, made ready to heave it back at us. Charley and I made ready to catch it if she did, standing knee-deep in the water. For a moment both parties stared at each other. Then, slowly, she let the thing drop from her hands and fall on the deck, looking exceedingly foolish.

"The kind of helpful passenger I don't like" Charley muttered to me as we put our backs under the curve of the bow again, "is the guy that pushes one way while you're bustin' your guts pushin' the other. At least she don't do that."

So we dismissed the incident, started "hup-hup"ing and "To-gether–now!"ing at each other, and were greatly surprised when we heard a little gasp and more splashing close beside us.

The water pouring over that bar was not only abominably cold, but fast as well–dangerous stuff to wade in if you are not used to it. The contours of a gravel bar represent a delicate balance between resistive forces and moveable objects. As soon as you place your foot on its surface you upset that balance, and vigorous movements at once begin both around and under your feet.

Charley and I left our places and started towards the girl. She hesitated, stood still, looked down. There's another danger on those bars: you can get a hazy view of the sand and pebbles streaming about your feet; you can see the water gliding swiftly over them. You learn further against the current than you need to. You may even get dizzy.

We reached her just as she fell, pulled her up before she got thoroughly wet, and boosted her back aboard.

"Start up the engine and change your clothes beside it" I told her. "It's warm there. We've got her moving. We'll be off in a few minutes."

She obeyed. Charley and I watched her enter the pilot-house with a bundle of clothes under her arm, then went to our lifting and shoving again. In about five minutes we had the *Lady* free.

We scrambled aboard, raced back to the pilot-house, called to Linda to put the engine in gear, and started nosing our way through the mess of shallows in which we found ourselves. Charley, at the wheel, bore down on the throttle, gently at first, then heavily, a look of vast surprise on his owlish features. The throttle was stuck. He bore down more heavily. Something gave. The engine let out a mighty roar, and we started to charge madly toward a bar directly in front of us. Charley threw the wheel over. I struggled to raise up on the throttle. It was stuck again, wide open now. It was stuck at the other end of the line, by the carburetor, down in the engine room which had recently become the *Lady*'s changing room. I shouted to Linda to free it. In the roar of the engine close beside her, she couldn't hear me.

Something had to be done, and quickly. If we hit at that speed, we'd never get off. One of us two men had to go down into the engine room and release that blasted lever. Charley and I didn't draw lots. I was married; he wasn't; I went down.

It was all right, I thought at first. She was almost fully dressed. Unfortunately, it was one of her wet stockings that had fallen on the throttle lever and jammed it; but at least I was able to say truthfully that the thing was in the habit of jamming itself anyway. I said so, and I looked up at her to say it, smiling reassuringly, I hoped. That was when I saw what I should not have seen; she was crying.

The tears I saw were tears of vexation, I suppose. Whatever they were, there was nothing I could do about them. I swopped shouts with Charley about the workability of the throttle now, smiled again, and bolted out the door.

In deep water five minutes later, tidying up our pushing-poles on the bow-deck, I noticed that our life-buoy was missing. Probably Charley had knocked it off as we clambered aboard, and certainly I should have checked to see that it was in its proper place the moment we got underway. If it hadn't have been for Linda I should not have turned back to get it, but I didn't like the responsibility of traveling with her aboard and not a single life-buoy on the boat.

We located it eventually half a mile below Charley's original bar. It had swung into an eddy below another bar, and was slowly circling there. We hit a bar trying to nose our way into it, backed off, tried another approach, hit again.

"Hold her there!" I yelled to Charley, and jumped overboard. It looked shallow all the way, but I had to go in clear to my arm-pits before I could lay my hands on the bobbing ring. By the time I got back to the boat I had some revised opinions on whose responsibility it was for all this waste of time, and I suppose I showed them. Linda was standing beside Charley in the pilot-house, warmly wrapped about and with her face freshly touched up. Right in front of her eyes I threw the life-buoy back in its proper place and securely tied it there. Then, in my turn, I hurried to the warmth of the engine room with a bundle of dry clothes under my arm.

By the time I re-emerged the Sans Sault was in sight, and Linda wasn't. I gathered from Charley that she had gone forward under the canvas and "didn't seem very happy about sump'n."

I had other worries on my mind. That name, Sans Sault, is a complete misnomer: as far as I could see in every direction the river ahead of us was full of falls. The steamboat channel through the rapids swung fairly close to the left bank, I knew; but I couldn't see it. I saw what I thought was a smoother and more direct channel wide enough for my boat near the middle of the stream. Standing on the bows with the sounding pole in one hand, I pointed the other in that direction.

The channel proved good for perhaps a quarter of a mile, rough, but deep, and not too fast for three-quarters throttle. Then my pole struck solidly against packed gravel– six feet deep on that first thrust. Six feet dwindled to five, to four, to three. Next there was the flat top of a pink rock visible right under our bows, a smooth curtain of water sliding over it. It was part of a ledge rising to a small water-licked island ten yards to port, forming a small cascade the same distance to starboard. I measured two foot six on top of the rock. The *Lady* drew two four at her deepest part astern. With luck we might make it.

We didn't make it. The bow passed over the ledge, the sheltered deck passed over; the waist; the engine room. Island and cascade crept slowly aft on either side. Then the rudders, or perhaps the steel shoe under the skeg, rubbed hard.

About us, as far as the water stretched in all directions, were movement and tumbling violence, orderly lines of gliding, curving, foaming waves that in one blink of the eye seemed to be continually rushing down the slope, in another to be perpetually charging up it. I could not understand why we alone stood motionless in all this motion. I kept waving to Charley to give the motor a little more juice and send us creeping ahead again.

84

Then, suddenly, the world was going around. The static picture of regimented white-caps eternally charging up a static slope, never getting anywhere, was static no longer. All the fixed lines of riffle and rapid were sliding askew, changing their angles to each other. The *Lady* was swinging quickly to starboard about her stern.

The small cascade was suddenly under my feet. I stabbed senselessly at the clearly visible ledge it poured over, sounding still, still automatically signaling my findings back to Charley. Two foot less a quarter I showed him, and immediately the bow struck, hard, throwing me to my knees on the deck.

I had taken us a quarter of an hour to gain a quarter mile up the narrow channel I had found. We slipped sidewise down it in less than three minutes. We hit sometimes in the bows, sometimes astern, at once slewing rapidly till we swung free. Sometimes we hit fair amidships. On the bow I straddled the mid-section of the canoe, holding it aboard with my legs, holding myself aboard with hands clutched to ropes and bollards. We heeled over till it seemed we must upset–over, over, over, till the upper gunnel made a high line against the cold blue sky. Then came a mighty lurch, a grinding, a series of bumps, a sudden righting, and smoothly we rode sidewise down the stream till we struck again.

We were free at last and floating clear in the deep water between the bars and the rapids proper. I looked back at Charley, smiled ruefully. He smiled ruefully at me. He pointed to the right of the channel I had first chosen. I nodded my head. He swung the boat's nose in that direction, then disappeared for a moment, doubtless going down into the engine room to see if we were taking any water there. That seemed a sound idea. I walked aft of the canvas and looked into the open space behind it.

The boat was all right, but Linda wasn't. We reached the open space at the same time. Tottering slightly, holding to the ridge pole as she came, she emerged from under the shelter, leaned weakly over-side, and was violently sick.

We never did find the steamboat channel through the Sans Sault. Instead we followed another promising lane nearer midstream till it was blocked by two boulders too close together for our passage between them. We angled over then towards the mouth of Mountain River, and after half an hour's touch-and-go playing with what

85

Charley called "snorters," reached smooth water. It's a new route I've marked on my charts, but I don't recommend it.

We were drawing near Norman Wells when I woke the next morning.

"No pancakes" said Linda weakly. "Charley says we can all get breakfast at the company hotel."

I raised myself on my elbows and looked about. Her bags were packed and standing neatly in a row.

"You're leaving us here?" I asked.

"You'd sooner I did, wouldn't you?"

I hesitated a moment; then "For your own sake–yes", I said.

She gave me no verbal reply to that. Her answer was in her face, but I could not interpret it. What she would have preferred to do at that time I still don't know.

After breakfast I went with her to the airport at the far end of the settlement.

"It's this way" the agent explained. "Lunky's got orders to take the *Peel* up to Bear River rapids three times, shuttling oil barges from here to there. Two weeks extra that will mean, and all his passengers are hollering. So the company's chartered the plane to take them out from here. Three trips extra they're making on the job. Then they won't be back till the next scheduled flight, two weeks from now."

"Miss Driver was originally a passenger on the *Peel*" I said. "She joined us at the Ramparts Rapids. She has the same rights to passage on the plane as the rest of them."

"Could be, and I guess if there was room they wouldn't make any bones about it. But there isn't. Every trip full. See?"

He showed me the lists. I noticed that the third was one name shorter than the other two, and pointed out the discrepancy.

"That's for Flocky, one of our own men, got a transfer to Wrigley airport" the agent said. "He ought to go on the first plane, but he's wiring for permission to take the third instead."

"Thanks" I said, and took Linda's arm as we went out the door. We watched our feet carefully as we circled a mud-puddle together.

"The *Peel* should be here by tonight," I said. "I'll wait till she arrives, if you wish. You'll have your old cabin back again, and the whole boat–"

We were around the puddle now. She stopped and faced me, her hand on my arm.

"There'll be a seat on that third plane from Wrigley south after what's-his-name gets off" she said. "Do you think you and the *Lady* can get me there in time?"

Put that way, I couldn't refuse her request, though I strained my engine and drive-gear to help her. The plain matter of fact was that it had been her own idea to transfer from the *Peel* to my boat, and she was determined not to transfer back again. That would be the same as admitting that she had made a mistake. She was a very selfish little thing, I thought; and at that time I was probably quite right in that judgement of her.

We reached Fort Norman that night, pulled out early the next morning, but not as early as we might have done. I had forgotten to try the Mission for a new propeller on my way down river in the spring. I spent three hours there this time, and was duly apologetic when I returned aboard.

"No prop there" I explained to Linda as we turned the *Lady*'s nose upstream and began to leave the white cone of Bear Rock behind us. It was snowing on that great height, and looked as if it would shortly be snowing all around us.

The hundred and fifty miles from Fort Norman to Wrigley took us five days–as miserable days as Linda, the weather, and the numerous short-comings of my boat could make them. None of these agencies was responsible, of course. The weather was the weather. The boat I should never have taken out of Aklavik in that condition. And Linda could no more help being what she was than a snowstorm could help being a snowstorm or the *Lady* could help being nothing more than a small scow with a wonky drive-assembly. Such philoso-phisings, however, did not prevent me secretly cursing all three at times.

Our unhappy tourist got few of the thrills she had been looking for on this trip. Instead she made a close acquaintance with dirt, cold, monotony, and anxiety. I am sure that from the second day out from Norman she looked forward to nothing else so much as to the day she would get off my boat and step aboard that plane southbound for hot baths and three-course meals. And, with the rest of us, she must have doubted at times whether we would make the airport in time to catch the plane.

She did her best to put up a pretense of cheerfulness. It was good, as I think of it now, but not good enough to fool a couple of experts on the subject like Charley and myself. Eventually her very presence huddled over the engine beside us to keep warm was enough to put both of us in the dumps as well.

Unexpectedly, Charley came to her defense.

"She's a good kid, Ken" he said. "I reckon the weather's getting her down, though. It ain't exactly what I asked for."

If Charley had asked for that weather, I'd have shot him. There is an old Cornish rhyme that kept recurring to me as we plugged along: "First it blew, then it snew, then it thew, then it frew–Orrid!" They must have fog in Cornwall, too: we had–a whole day of it while we lay alongside a small sand island with nothing more interesting on it than the skeleton of a long-dead fish. The shelters I had rigged on the *Lady* proved quite inadequate to keep that kind of weather where it belonged.

We might all have forgiven the boat her poor accommodations if she had run well. She didn't. Through all the sixty-six miles of fast water from Old Fort Point to Blackwater River we never dared run at more than three-quarter throttle. The three-sixty-fourths of an inch of wobble in her shaft obviously couldn't become worse of itself, but its effects could become more noticeable–and they did, daily. A continual groaning and shuddering rose from the deadwood in which the shaft turned, more urgent every mile we traveled.

There was only one thing to do–to stand behind the wheel and watch the clay slopes of the banks, the myriad stones of the beaches, the weary trees leaning far outstream, creep slowly, slowly, by. We gave Linda her turns at the wheel in the better places, but she lacked experience to judge fast water from slow, deep from shallow, and neither Charley nor I could find words to describe those minute differences of ripple and flow, changing with every change of light, of sun's angle (when there was any), of wind's breath, which distinguish one from the other. So we took the wheel from her, rough in our haste sometimes, or stood beside her, pointing the channel. To discomfort and anxiety, she must have added a sense of uselessness aboard, growing steadily through all the five days of the journey.

Forty or fifty mud-chinked log houses, one white-painted group of clapboard buildings, three broken-backed canoes upturned on the beach, and two black ravens flapping dismally from one snow-covered drift-log to another–that was Wrigley the morning we arrived there. Unreasonably, the sun was shining. I can't understand why the sun should ever bother to shine on Wrigley–unless it's for Mike's sake.

In the largest of the white-painted building we met him

"That's my first name" he said. "I won't tell you my last name because I'm the only guy in the North can get it around his tongue without needing an operation afterwards. It's furrin–Polish or Woppish or something. What can I do for you?"

We bought groceries, and asked for mail. Mike was postmaster as well as fur-trader. He was also the local doctor–at least he had the only medical supplies there–and combined in his one person the local representatives of the Department of Indian Affairs, the Department of Transport, and the principle northern airline. In addition, he operated the settlement's short-wave set, and, as he said, quite frequently "baptized and undertook." He was the only white man there. "I won all the prizes at the last Dominion Day celebration" he said.

He had good news for us. The plane had been stormbound at the Wells, and wouldn't reach Wrigley airport, twelve miles upstream, till three that afternoon. He set his radio panel-board buzzing while we watched him, talked with the plane, confirmed that Flocky's seat would be empty from the airport south. He was delighted to sell Linda a ticket then–it was the first one he'd sold in two years of business. With normal luck she'd sleep in Simpson that night, and reach Edmonton for supper the next day. She was pleased; he was pleased; I found it difficult to hide my satisfaction. I'd never take another woman aboard the *Lady*.

"You can make the airport in two hours from here" Mike said. "Come and have dinner with me before you pull out."

It was a fine new house he showed us into then, with cement sidewalks, and, of all conveniences unexpected, hot running water. Linda had a bath while I wrote a letter to Barbara and Charley peeled spuds.

It turned out during the meal that Mike was worried, that is, Mike the Indian Affairs man.

"Young squaw, Celestine Legentilhomme, came down from upriver to have a baby two weeks ago. Not very strong yet, not fit to travel by kicker and canoe. I'm looking for some way to sent her back."

He looked pointedly at me. I developed strong interest in a fox-hunting print hung on the wall opposite.

"You know what these people are" he said. "She's desperate to get back to her own folks. God knows why, but she is."

There was no denying the appeal in his eyes.

"The baby?" I asked.

"Oh, no worry there. We buried it yesterday."

"How far, Mike?"

"River Between Two Mountains last time she saw them. Thirty miles. Hell—you'll be there this time tomorrow. I'm sorry, Ma'am, I meant 'Shucks'."

I'd made a mistake when I took Linda aboard. I'd never asked Charley's opinion.

"How about it, Charley?"

Charley swallowed corn-beef hurriedly, gulped once.

"What I'm wondering about" he said, "is what gear she's got to sleep in. Some of these Indians don't carry much, and it's pretty damn cold on that boat, nights." Suddenly he squared his shoulders. "Aw hell! it's only one night—she can have my robe if she needs it."

Mike beamed on us then, and brought out the bottle he had been saving for Christmas.

Linda walked down to the boat with me while the others went to fetch the invalid aboard. Linda was thoughtful.

"You never asked how much you'd get paid for this" she said.

"I never thought of that" I answered, truthfully. Probably Mike would bring me a cheque from one or other of the Departments. Probably he wouldn't. It didn't matter if he didn't. I said so. I said also that I had better get busy cleaning out her cubby under the bows, ready for the new passenger, and she had better get busy packing her bags. She annoyed me then, she was so slow with the job, pausing every few minutes to gaze at the desolate mud walls of Wrigley. Myself, I could take in the whole scene in one glance.

Charley and Mike brought the Indian woman to the beach by dog-team, hallooing boyishly at the lead-dog which exhibited all the usual perversity of his kind. Charley carried her aboard, then came aft, started the engine, ran it till the water was hot, and thoroughly scrubbed his hands.

My God, Ken, she had a baby."

"So I understand" I said.

"What I mean is–well, hell, they can't be very choosey, the men in her tribe, can they?"

I agreed with him. Celestine was a flat-faced, lumpy-cheeked, slightly slant-eyed creature. She was about twenty-five, I guessed, but might have passed for forty anywhere except among her own people. Her clothes were filthy, redolent of the smoke and grease of many a forgotten camp-fire. By this time tomorrow Charley's robe, I thought, would be crawling.

I was wrong there. Linda had a better robe, bought at Norman Wells expressly for this trip. She had spread it in the cubby she had vacated, and when I looked inside I saw her covering the Indian woman's emaciated frame with it. A nice gesture, I thought, but I could think of a nicer one. Obviously she'd have no further use for the robe after she quit my boat; I'd been rather hoping she'd leave it to me.

Duty-bound, I went under the canvas to take a closer look at the woman, to examine the arrangements made for her comfort. Then I went ashore, untied the line, and stood with it in my hand, talking to Mike.

"Look, Mike–do you think that girl will be alive when we get there tomorrow?"

"I don't know" he answered frankly. "I figure if she's going to die, she'd be happier doing it among her own people–and far less trouble to us. But you never know with these people. She went hunting rabbits yesterday. Didn't do her any good, of course; but it just shows you. They're damn resilient, you know. If you hit a sandbar and need an extra hand to push you off–anything like that–you may get a surprise. They say she's a good cook, too."

Mike knew these natives better than I did. I shook his hand, pushed the bow clear, and clambered aboard.

As I was going aft Linda came out from under the canvas and called me down beside her.

"Ken, that woman should be in a hospital."

"She'll be on the beach thirty miles upriver this time tomorrow. I only hope her people are still there."

"Where's the nearest hospital, Ken?"

"Simpson. Hundred and fifty miles. Five days for us. I'm not taking her there."

91

She started to say something more, but I turned away, leaned over the gunnel, and waved good-bye to Mike's lone figure diminishing on the beach behind us. He might know more about the original owners of my beloved North than I did; but I had had some previous experience with them too. I wasn't doing this for the Indian girl's sake at all. I was doing it for Mike.

A few miles above Wrigley airport the Mackenzie gets fast again. Six to seven miles an hour, the charts say, but I'm sure they scamp the truth. Even with a bent shaft and a propeller that looks like a cubist's impression of a hangover the *Lady* can make eight miles an hour at three-quarter throttle, but she couldn't make that second point above the airport unless I opened the engine full out.

Charley didn't want me to do that. He offered to go ashore with the track-line and see whether he couldn't pull us over that riffle without my straining our driving gear. I wouldn't listen to him. I was happy and confident that night. I bore down on the throttle and kept it down for half an hour. So we rounded the point at last, got into a small bay above it–and I was just easing up when there came a ripping and a banging from under my feet, and immediately after the sound of water pouring in from astern.

We nosed ashore in a hurry, passed a line under the rudder, put block and tackle to it, and got the stern skidded up on a long drift log in fifteen of the busiest minutes any of us had ever lived through. She was safe then, her shattered deadwood six inches above water and her bows deep in it, all askew. That done, Charley and I set to work by flashlight to examine the damage. We saw soon that there was nothing for it but to whittle a new piece of deadwood out of the hardest wood we could find, to bore an inch and a half hole through it somehow, to bolt it onto the torn timbers as best we could–a two day job at least, and an unsatisfactory one at that. Simpson was an eight day journey now, if we could reach it at all.

We knocked off then, and stumbled through the rain towards the fire burning brightly fifty feet up the beach. It wasn't only raining that night: it was snowing too, freezing a bit, and thawing at the same time. The beach was the muddiest we had seen yet: we lost a boot each on the way to the campfire. And of course all our best heaving on the tackle hadn't raised the *Lady*'s stern high enough for us to work under it without squatting in two feet of slush and water, each one colder than the other.

We made jokes about these things. If we were depressed, we didn't let on. It was just like old times aboard the *Lady*.

As we approached the leaping fire we saw bedding and clothes strung on lines to dry about it. This new woman we had in our party was still too frail a body, still too ignorant of our particular mode of navigation on the Mackenzie, to take the place of another man in our crew; yet she had seen at once what part in the crisis she could play most usefully, and had set to it with astonishing good will and efficiency. She was an entirely different creature from that useless and melancholy thing we had brought from the Ramparts Rapids to Wrigley Airport.

Nearing the fire, we heard her voice ring out, singing one of those primitive, throbbing tunes her people cherish for reasons men like me will never understand. As a song I didn't think much of it, but I was delighted to hear it nevertheless, to hear the happiness in it, the confidence, the grand cheerfulness of that voice rising over the present discomfort and the bleak prospects of the situation in which we all found ourselves together.

I was delighted, yes–but not surprised. Linda had been like that ever since she gave her ticket to the Indian woman and sent her in her place on the plane to the hospital at Simpson.

Chapter 10

The Lady Goes in Reverse

It snowed and blew all night, snowed and blew all morning. The wind came from the north and had no gusts in it, no slacking off and no increase in the steady force with which it pushed upriver. Out in the middle of the stream the unseen waves must have strode in tumbling lines right-angled to the currents so exactly did directions of wind and valley coincide.

Only in the bay in which the boat was beached were they visible; there they rolled lazily shoreward, heavy with the slush they bore. White was land and sky; sullen grey the water; only a long line of black lay each way along the curve of the bay, where the waves washed snow off the mud, receded, and advanced again upon it.

About noon I crawled reluctantly from my sleeping-bag and went down to the beach, clambered over the gunnels, carefully moved about the interior of my little scow. There was two feet of water over the lower deck in her bows. There was six inches of snow weighting down the canvas stretched on a ridge-pole over her waist. There was a ten inch rectangular hole in her bottom where the planking began its curve under the engine room astern. Lying as she was, her nose deep in the water, her after end drawn as far up the beach as two men and woman could drag it with the aid of blocks and tackle, the *Lady* looked as if she would never move again.

I stood in the pilot house and looked through the open doorway. I had a better view of the bay than I had had the night before. A vast eddy circled in it, its nearer course driving the roiled water swiftly upstream along the shore, its outer limits hidden by the pall of slanting snow. Shoals and mud-bars lay in it also: those shoreward rolling waves were broken often, twisted awry, before they flung themselves wearily on the curving line of mud. At the lower end of the bay a long spit of gravel pointed far outstream, causing first a little rapids, then a riffle, then fast water. It was a bad spot, I thought, and we were lucky to be by it, even though in climbing the fast water we had shattered the dead-wood in which the *Lady*'s shaft revolved.

I ran back to the camp, ankle-deep in mud and snow. The sound of my axe, the tang of wood-smoke, wakened the sleepers. When Linda stirred I went quickly to her and brushed the snow from the coverings about her face. I would have done as much for Charley, but he was already up by the time I had helped Linda to her feet. They rose from their sleeping-bags fully dressed in the oddly assorted garments that the previous nigh's adventure had left dry. They joined me about the fire.

Well?"

It was Charley's voice, but it was to Linda's upturned face that I answered.

"I think we're beat" I said. "This weather's got me scared. It might freeze up any time. And even if it doesn't, looking at the whole situation this morning, looking at it as honestly as I can, I don't see any possibility of continuing upstream. We're beat."

They both stared at me. A slice of bacon drooped limply from one of Linda's hands. Charley held a small spruce tree in one of his, the hatchet in the other. Motionless as statues, stopped dead at the tasks they had been working on, they stared at me.

"What I propose" I said, "is to shove her back in and drift downstream. I'll let you fellows off at Wrigley airport if you wish, to wait for the next plane or for the *Peel* to take you out of this blasted country. Myself, I want to drift her as far as Norman if I can. There's a capstan and horses there. I'll be able to pull her out, safe for the winter."

"Whatever you say, Ken."

Again it was Charley's voice, tired and resigned now, and again Linda's eyes, not resigned at all. I could not get away from those great blue eyes staring at me in wonder and disappointment, in effort to understand.

"As a precaution" I said," and since we'll have to lie up here till the wind dies anyway, I suppose we ought to whittle some sort of new deadwood for that blasted crooked shaft to turn in, and shove the blasted wonky prop back on again. But once we get out into mid-stream we'll just drift, saving what power we've got for emergencies."

Linda spoke at last.

"Downstream, Ken?"

"Downstream, Linda. Boats don't drift upstream. It's been tried, but it's never been made to work yet–not in this country."

Her eyes grew puzzled again, then brightened.

"But supposing when the job is done the boat should happen to work as well as before–what then?" she asked.

"It won't" I said. "There isn't a hope. There isn't a chance of our making even a half-decent job of her on this beach. We need lathes, forges, a whole workshop of tools. We need hardwood of some kind to replace the hunk that shaft has torn out of her. We need some to straighten that shaft. If we put that thing back in as it is we'll just have the same old trouble all over again–and perhaps not be so near shore next time it happens."

"But–"

"Oh, what's the use, Linda? Without help of some kind the three of us can't even haul her stern high enough out of the water to let us work at it properly. We're beat."

That silenced them both. Charley raised his axe, let it fall against a branch of the small tree, let the branch fall to his feet. Linda poured flap-jack batter in the frying pan.

After breakfast Charley went down to the boat. He took the hand-pump from the engine-room, installed it forward, and began a steady grind of moving its handle up and down. He sang as he worked, bearing down on the handle with the first word of each verse.

"*Be* pleased to check your chewing gum
With Rastus at the door,
And I'll tell you bible stories
Like you've never heard before."

Charley always sang when things were going badly with the *Lady*, always the same song.

Under the shelter of a tarpaulin angled against the wind, Linda and I talked.

"The plain fact of the matter is," I said, "it's not the boat, not the time of year, not the Mackenzie River, that doomed this trip to failure from the beginning. It's myself."

She was trying hard to understand me, trying to put herself in my place, and, poor little rich man's daughter that she was, finding it very difficult to do so.

"What do you mean, Ken?"

"I haven't got what it takes for this kind of job, Linda. I'm nervous–not physically, but in a penny-pinching sort of way. I can stand up to rapids and sandbars all right, but when it comes to repairs of the boat's machinery I've always been content to put things back as they were rather than run the risk of ruining them entirely by trying to improve them."

"That's not entirely penny-pinching" she said. "I think I'd feel the same in this country, knowing how long it takes to get new parts or to find someone who can mend a broken piece for you."

"All right, if it's not penny-pinching it's something worse" I countered. "It's plain stupidity. Just because you can't easily get repairs done for you in this country, you should never start out on a trip like this till you're sure every item of your motive power is as near perfect as it can be made. When those fellows were straightening my shaft for me in Aklavik I should have let them stay with the job till they hammered the last three sixty-fourth of an inch of wobble out of the end of it–or else never have started on this trip. It was the same with the prop. I spent hours and hours filing it before I went to Tuk, hours and hours filing it after I got back to Aklavik. That helped, of course, gave her more speed–but what that prop needs is somebody with courage enough to wang it about with a hammer and be damned if breaks off a blade or so. They're all bad; one's very bad. I think I may have caused as much vibration as ever the shaft did."

"But you did try to get a new prop, didn't you, Ken?"

"Sure, looked all over the country, got into more arguments than I met in six years of war. She's left-handed, you see, direct drive from the engine, and most of them on small boats are right-handed, using a reduction gear that swings them counter to the engine. Most fellows down here have never seen a left-handed one before; some of

97

them couldn't believe their eyes when I showed them mine. It took me two days to convince one fellow that I didn't have it on backwards, that it wouldn't make any difference if I did have. Finally I wired out to Edmonton, hoping that one could be sent down to me by plane before I left Aklavik. It came too, just in time, just what I wanted, except for one trifling item–brand new, right taper, right size, right pitch–AND–right-handed. Some damn fool–"

"It's no use at all, Ken?"

"No use at all, Linda. Oh I could use it all right if I was content to run stern-first all the way to Fort Nelson. Even I've got sense enough not to try that. It's up in the bow now. I'm taking it out with me even if I have to go by plane and pay a dollar a pound freight on it. I'm going to wrap it around that damn clerk's neck, then ask for my money back–and get it too."

I lit a cigarettes then, and puffed savagely on it, angry at that stupid pen-pusher in Edmonton, at the ill-luck that had plagued me all summer, at myself most of all. Linda talked on, with many pauses between her word, trying to comfort me, to cheer me, handicapped in that task by the very success of her previous effort to understand me. I think she realised better even than I did how much it pained me to give up this madman's exploit on which I had set my heart.

Charley ran out of new verses for his song and settled down to a steady repetition of the last line of his favourite:

"*And* the whale it did the rest." Clank, swoosh.
"*And* the whale it did the rest." Clank, swoosh.

The wind abated a little, and the snow ceased falling, the sun glared fleetingly through a curtain of red cloud above the far side of the river; and from the upstream lay of the beach a dog came trotting through the snow towards us. I thought the great shaggy beast was a wolf at first. Certainly I never saw in it the forerunner of our salvation.

Jake and Izor, trappers on their way down river by canoe to their base cabin on the East Branch of the Mackenzie, had put in out of the wind the night before, and were camped around the point half a mile above us. They had made a good muskrat hunt the previous spring, had flown to Edmonton by the first plane after breakup, had spent nearly all their money in the city, and were returning for another hard winter's labour by the cheapest means available. It was an old story, I thought when I heard it first, different from most only in that they had saved enough of their fur money to buy two good canoes and some supplies before they started north, and to acquire the raw materials for a good dog-team on the way downriver. The Alberta Government, via the Liquor Control Board in this case, had not got it all.

Then I heard the true story. Jake had brown eyes and a grey beard, Izor grey eyes and a brown beard (and an immense nose on him, dwarfing his other features); they also had a pair of black eyes with them, shining little black eyes set in a bright little brown face, perky and smiling. "Snippet" they called the boy sometimes, sometimes "Pipsqueak"–or any one of a host of other affectionate nicknames. Alfred Peter 'Iggins was his proper name, and he had been born and raised in Stepney, London, England. He was twelve years old. When he was about six, he guesses, although he had not been told till two years later, his father had been burned to crisp in a tank near Bardia. When he was nine a V-bomb had wiped out his mother and three sisters, leaving only him and Aunt Priscilla alive. Somehow or other–I never got the rights of it–Jake and Izor heard about young Alfred Peter 'Iggins. They wrote Aunt Priscilla. Aunt Priscilla, though grieved, thought it all for the best in the short and the long, and probably the Lord's will besides. So Jake and Izor sent a large part of their winter's fur money overseas, and in due time had delivered to them by plane one small boy. They bought him a .22 rifle, winter clothes, a case of school-books, a super-super Meccano set and seventy-five dollars and eighty-three cents worth of concentrated cod-liver oil and vitamin pills. Then they all headed north together.

One way or another this business had run into a good bit more money than they had thought it would. They didn't regret spending it, not for a moment; but it was a pity, Jake thought, that it had knocked on the head another project they had in mind when they set out for civilisation that spring. The whole purpose of the expedition had been to pick them out a suitable wife for Izor. For his part, Izor did not seem at all grieved that events had turned out as they had. He blushed, then recovered.

"Instead, we got Limey-boy" he said, "gettin' fat, ain't he?'

He was, and no wonder. They had put the kettle on when they

99

saw me following the dog towards them. We ate now. My first impression at the meal was that they simply tyrannized, in a benevolent sort of way, that unfortunate boy. They had killed a mule-deer swimming the river the day before, and seemed determined that he should consume every morsel of it before it went bad. Three times they heaped his plate with a man's portion, insisted on his eating every scrap of it, watching him as fondly as if they were feeding all the starving children in Europe, then let him of his own accord dig into the bannock and strawberry jam. I thought he was going to burst.

However, that first impression of mine was quite wrong. I heard their story, they heard mine: then they both turned to Alfie.

"What do you say, Kid-wump?" Jake asked, beaming down at the boy. "Do we give the man a hand, or don't we? You're the boss in this here gang."

At some period early in the war young 'Iggins had been evacuated from London, had got into the wrong social batch somehow, and had picked up odd phrases curiously contrasted to his own normal aitch-miserly speech.

"Oh, rawther" he said, accenting both syllables.

Early the next morning Jake, Izor, Alfie, and their seven dogs came down to help us. We had three sets of double blocks and tackle strung out on the beach, giving us an effective strength, I reckoned, of forty-eight men, twelve women, and twelve boys, not counting the dogs. Consequently I didn't see that we needed to use the team; but all the impassioned eloquence of Demosthenes would not have sufficed to persuade Jake to forego this first chance to demonstrate his skill with them to Alfie. For their part, the dogs welcomed another chance: they hadn't been able to have a decent go at one another's throats all the way down river in the canoes and thought this a grand opportunity to start deciding which one was going to be the boss of the pack. Jake handled them: Charley, Linda, and I heaved and ho'd on a line alongside them; and Izor splashed boldly into the water outside the boat and started prying between skid-log and the *Lady*'s planking with the most suitable object he found handy. The boat stuck, then came with a rush, two feet for the twenty-four feet of mud that we all stumbled through before we fell flat on our faces.

It was while the lines were being run out for a new purchase that I noticed what had seemed to Izor the most suitable thing handy for prying under the boat. It was the *Lady*'s drive-shaft.

I didn't let Izor know how I felt about that. I wanted to talk to Linda about it, and Izor couldn't come within ten feet of her without blushing 'til that great nose of his glowed like a soldering iron. I didn't let Linda know quite how I felt about it either.

"That's done it" I said. "The only way to get a straight piece out of that shaft now would be to saw it up in little pieces, starting with two feet off the coupling end."

Linda took me seriously.

"And move the engine two feet aft" she said. "You know, Ken, if you did that, you could run the exhaust pipes out astern and not get nearly so many fumes inside. Have you ever thought of doing that?"

I had. Once I had even gone so far as to try to loosen the pipes to add new fitting to them. Heat had virtually welded them together, however; I hadn't been able to budge the joints.

"Two foot six" I said. "Damn Izor!"

"Shhh!" Linda's warning was a little late. Alfie, aimlessly walking towards us, was already within hearing distance, and must surely have heard my opinion of one of his gods.

"I think two feet would do it" she said. "And look, surely the rest of it is perfectly straight."

"Well maybe. But there's still those exhaust pipe joints. We can't even get them out the old holes unless we change the angle right where they come out of the jackets."

"If we could only heat them–" she began.

"If we ran the engine, Linda, with no water in it, just for a minute–"

"That might do it" she agreed.

After men and dogs had got the stern a full foot clear of the ground, we tried it. Linda was more nervous than I.

"Shut it off, Ken. You'll burn out the valves!"

I braced my foot against the far gunnel and pulled as hard as I could on the pipe wrench. I couldn't move it.

"Give her more throttle" I said.

Iridescent colours began to play across the elbow between the jaws of my wrench, heat began to creep up the handle to my palms. I stuck a two-foot piece of pipe over the end, braced myself, and pulled again. The pipe moved toward me this time, slowly, then with a rush. Linda cut the switch while I was picking myself up off the

101

deck.

The next man's job was the shaft. For the first time, I had qualms.

"I don't like this" I said, as Linda handed me the hacksaw. "It's so final."

"Pinny-pinching again?" Linda asked.

I started to saw.

Another big job was to cut a key-way in the shortened shaft, with no more adequate tools than the hack-saw and a half-inch cold chisel. I left that to Linda's direction.

"Charley'll do the heavy work on that if you'll show him how" I said, and outlined quickly a number of smaller jobs that I wanted her to do, to adjust wiring, throttle-control, and water-hose to the new position the engine would take. She didn't mind: those pettifogging details were what she had always got assigned to her when she was a mechanic in the Spars, she said, but–

"But, Heavens, Ken, you're in a hurry."

"I'm in one stream-lined hell of a hurry" I agreed, and departed. I could not tell her why, because little Alfie had joined us in the cabin.

Jake, Izor, and Charley were talking on the beach.

"I'm off to rustle up something for the new deadwood" I said to Charley.

Jake turned toward me.

"Charley here says you want a piece of hard stuff, Mr. Conibear."

I agreed. With spruce in her, which was the best I could hope to find on the beach, I would drift down river, largely at the mercy of wind and current; with hardwood, I might be able to run the engine all the way to Norman.

"Go on up to the camp" Jake said. "I'll be right behind you."

He had to assemble and untangle his dogs before he could start. I was too impatient to wait there. Waiting ten minutes at the men's camp instead, I grew still more impatient. I was desperately anxious to get all these repair jobs done that day, to pull out that night if possible, not for my own sake but for young Alfie's. Life for him under the wings of these great-hearted but impractical foster-uncles of his would be full of blessings, but full of hardships too. In prospect the very hardships might appeal to him more than the blessings, and by the look of the boy I judged that he would be able

102

to endure them well enough once he was gradually broken in to them. But he was in no condition to meet them yet, physically or morally. It would be a poor start in his new life, I thought, if his party should get frozen in a three or four day trudge along the beach above their base-cabin. And I would never forgive myself if I was the cause of such a thing happening.

The storm, dying now, was a warning. Winter was coming here, creeping up from the north. Winter was nearer down on the East Branch. Every minute possible Jake, Izor, and Alfie should be paddling, putting the long miles behind them. That was the cause of my hurry.

By the time Jake joined me I had tramped a ten foot walk of impatience up and down on the mud of the beach. He led me straight to the freighter canoe drawn half its length out of the water.

"Bought a lot of junk before we heard of Alfie-boy" he said. "Kinda had some idees about how we was going to fix the place up nice for the little lady we hoped to get for Izor, you see. You know how most trapper's cabins are, skinnin and stretchin done inside, pelts hangin on stretchers over the stove, fur and innards right on the table beside you when you eat."

He worked as he talked, tugging at the canvas that covered the goods in the canoe, poking about in the bows, saying "No, ain't here", moving to the waist, repeating "No, tain't here", going on with his explanation all the time.

In forethought for the comfort of the unknown bride, Jake and Izor had built a special skinning cabin apart from the one they lived in at their base-camp. "Fixed her up nice, stove in her and everything." Then it occurred to them that they might as well do their butchering in it too– that vast amount of cutting up caribou carcasses for dog-feed and personal use which makes a large part of the nightly chores of every trapper. The building of this special cabin was the last work they had done before they left their base in the spring: the fitting out of it was the first item of business they had turned to when they reached the city. One by one old Jake brought out cleavers, meat-saw, knives, stones, and showed them to me; then came at last to the object of his search–the first butcher's chopping block I'd ever seen in the Northwest Territories.

Grunting, he straightened up with it in his arms, grunting passed it over to me, grunting, I clung to it, bending at the knees.

"Maple, I think" he said. "Hard stuff anyways. She'll do you."

My protests were useless. My objections that it would takes me three days to whittle the thing down to the size I wanted were silenced when he produced a swede-saw with three spare blades.

I hurried back to the *Lady*, made measurements, gathered up Linda and a three foot length of inch pipe, hurried to the upriver camp again. Jake had most of the sawing done by the time we arrived. I heated my steel pipe till it was cherry red, moved it quickly with gloved hands, jammed it upright between two drift-logs, pressed the middle of the block heavily on the heated end, guided by Linda's eye and voice. Jake watched us awhile, then ambled off downriver.

It took us about an hour to burn the hole through that block, but it was neat and true when it was done. We hurried off with it.

As we neared the *Lady* we heard a chiming of metal on metal coming from our own camp.

"That's Jake and Izor a'thrash'n and a'pound'n on the prop" Charley explained. "They didn't seem to think she looked quite right somehow."

"Good Lord!" I exclaimed, dropped the block, and started to run. Linda stopped me.

"They can't make it any worse, Ken."

"They can break a blade off–"

"What that prop needs" she interrupted, "is somebody with courage enough to wang it about with a hammer and be damned. That's what you said yourself."

"Hammer?" said Charley. "Them guys, they're using a axe."

I laughed then. It didn't matter if they smashed the thing to pieces: I'd drift. I would probably drift anyway.

I didn't see the propeller when Jake and Izor came back with it and put it on the shaft. I was working inside the boat with Linda. Charley tended a small fire hard by the *Lady*'s side, heating six inch spikes in it, passing them to Alfie in a tin can. Alfie passed the can through the porthole, his small hand momentarily visible. Linda took it from him, grasped the hot spikes one by one in pliers, and passed them to me, carefully avoiding contact with the slightly leaky gasoline line. I burnt holes through the ship's timbers and into the deadwood from either side, put bolts in them when they met, lag-screws when they didn't. Finally I caulked the joint, then shouted to the men on shore to start prying us into the water again. By the time we got ashore to help with a final heave, the propeller was sliding into the waves.

I got a brief glimpse of it, couldn't believe my eyes and shouted to 'vast heaving. I was too late: the *Lady*'s stern kept moving, and in the lap of the waves about them the three bronze blades took on a thousand different shapes each more improbable than the ones I thought I had seen. In the general shouting and heaving my shout passed unnoticed, and I was content to say nothing more about the matter. It was too late anyway–and surely I'd been mistaken.

She floated, my *Lady*, responsive again to every least shift of weight, alive. We hurried aboard and went to work in the engine room again. I never before saw a line-up job come as sweetly as that one did then. When we were done Linda could turn the shaft with one hand.

I poled the stern around till the boat lay at right angles to the beach, and yelled to the men ashore.

"Going to give her a try, fellows."

Charley and Alfie came aboard. Jake and Izor, coming from the camp with the last of our gear, threw it aboard, but themselves stayed ashore.

Linda had already started the engine. I went below and gently eased the lever into gear ahead. At once the shaft began to spin, smoothly, sweetly, like a piece of oiled silk turning. Wider and wider I opened the throttle, faster and faster the shaft spun. Never in all the time I'd owned the boat had that drive assembly turned with so little vibration. I couldn't feel so much as a tremor in the stuffing box when I rested my hand upon it.

Linda and I looked up together. Our eyes met, gleaming. Then quickly she turned hers away and glanced out the porthole.

"Ken! We're moving!"

"That's all right" I said. "She won't climb very far on that skid. She'll push off easy."

"But we're not moving ahead, Ken! We're moving astern, fast!"

That was when I knew that I had been seeing straight when I looked at that propeller as it had slid into the water.

I got to the wheel in three jumps, and shoved it hard over. We were about a hundred feet from shore, backing through a mess of mud-bars towards the fast water beyond the bay. I eased up on the throttle, swing the wheel the other way, bore down on the throttle, swing the wheel again. Nothing seemed to make any difference: the *Lady* never had steered worth a milquetoast cuss when going astern, and with this particular prop she seemed to move as fast, or as slow, with the engine idling as with the throttle wide open. The little rapids drew close astern, waves washing greedily over it. And at that moment, Alfie came sliding along the gunwale toward the pilot-house.

"Put her in gear ahead–you know what I mean" I said to Linda.

She caught on quick. I suppose she had already guessed what had been done to us. She slipped the engine into reverse. Immediately we started to move ahead, helped by the eddy swinging into the bay, but still drifting sidewise towards the rapids. I bore down on the throttle then. The motor roared, a great fountain of froth burst out astern, and we began to move slowly up the inside channel in the curve of the bay–slowly, that is, except for the six-knot reverse current that hustled us through that channel.

Probably Alfie didn't know about that current, and thought we were making this quite creditable speed against one flowing in the opposite direction. Anyway, he was greatly impressed by that huge tumultuous bubbly wake we threw up stern.

In the few weeks he had been in the country that kid had managed to pick up a fair amount of Canadian lingo to add to his strangely mixed English.

He looked at the wake, then looked at me, with shining eyes.

"Gee! Gosh!" he exclaimed. "Jake and Izor shore fixed that prop for you, didn't they?"

I know my Canadian lingo too, a little better than Alfie.

"Yes, son" I agreed, "they shore fixed her."

"Aw, we're all right, nothing to worry about now, Izor" said Charley. "Good-bye".

"You'll write to me, Alfie-boy, won't you? Promise" said Linda. "Tell me all about the deer you shoot, the fun you have driving the dogs. Good-bye." And she kissed him.

"Jake" I said, "I'll bring you down a case of oranges when I come next spring. I'd never have got out of this hole if you fellows hadn't come along. Good-bye."

We waited till they had quite disappeared from sight around the point, then got blocks and tackle out again and pulled the *Lady*'s stern up on the beach till we could work at her driving gear without getting more than our knees wet. The job we did there took about ten minutes. Then we pushed her in again and proceeded upriver.

With only an hour's running time left that night, we made ten miles, against fast water all the way. Every inch of that ten miles was a pleasure. There wasn't a tremor of excess vibration under our feet, we no longer had fumes in the engine room to spoil the comfort we drew from the motor's warmth, and we threw out a wash each side of us that rocked drift logs on the muddy beaches a mile behind us. The *Lady* ran better than I'd known her to run before.

I'll never get my money back on the right-handed propeller that blasted idiot of a clerk in Edmonton sent to me at Aklavik. But for Jake and Izor I might have, I think; they quite spoilt my plans. I'm no mechanic, and if they hadn't done their great-hearted ignorant best to hammer my old left-handed prop into a right-handed one I would never have thought of putting the new one on and running the rest of the way forward with my shaft turning in reverse gear.

Chapter 12

The Lady Observes The Traditions

The *Lady Greenbelly* ploughed steadily up the middle of the Mackenzie River. No longer was it necessary to seek the slacker current close inshore, to add a full mile sometimes to the direct course up a reach simply because in its bays the water flowed possibly two miles an hour slower than it did in midstream. Instead I pointed my small scow's nose straight up mid-channel and watched the green and yellow shores, the brown beaches, the grey drift-logs on them, slip more rapidly astern than they had done for many days before. I had much to be grateful for that morning, and I was.

With that new thrust under her counter, the *Lady* rode very smoothly, brushing aside the little waves she overtook as matters quite insignificant to a creature of her strength. When, about an hour after the sun winked over the eastern shore, I felt her lurch a little, first to one side, then to the other, I knew at once that there was movement other than me aboard her. Happy little family that we were, I could even judge by the size and feel of the lurches which of my two shipmates it was who was causing them.

I got the blackened lard-pail from its nail, dumped equal quantities of cocoa, sugar, and powdered milk into it, and set the pail on that spot of the pilot-house deck where hitherto one minute's vibration from below had always sufficed to make a perfect mixture of the three. This morning it didn't work; there was almost no vibration. I beat the stuff about with a spoon, holding the wheel with one hand, gazing ahead at the water streaming towards the bows and at the inverted V of the canvas shelter forward of the engine-room.

I had been quite right. In a moment Linda's head appeared in the V, her mass of golden hair tousled and wind-blown. She looked a while first out one side, then out the other, happily; then stepped up the port gunnel and came aft along it. That little nose of hers was quite shiny this morning, and her lips had only their own natural pink to colour them. She gave me a friendly smile and a cheerful good-morning. I passed her the lard-pail. She drew hot water from the engine, brought tin cups, filled them.

"What about breakfast?" she asked.

"We'll stop at the mouth of River Between Two Mountains in about half an hour" I said. "Should have a word with Celestine's people if they're still there. If not, the way she's running now, we can afford to take time out to warm up a little something on the beach anyway."

"The way she's running now" Linda repeated thoughtfully. "Ken, how far is it to Simpson?"

"About a hundred mile. And about another hundred from there up the Liard to Fort Nelson—good going after you get past the rapids, if you don't have engine trouble. I know what you're thinking about."

I did, too. With the right-handed propeller on her shaft, and with the gears set in reverse to drive her ahead, it was working splendidly, and there were no indications of trouble with the engine's gear-box yet; but they were bound to come. Linda, with experience in the Spars making her a far better mechanic than ever I will be, had said the night before that any gear system is sure to wear badly if run in reverse indefinitely.

"I've been thinking of it this morning" I assured her. "I'm going to see old Quillian about it as soon as we reach Simpson."

"Quillian? Who's he?"

"Mighty smart fellow, Linda. One of the best men with small boats anywhere on the Mackenzie. He may have a left-handed prop that would do us, though that's unlikely. He didn't have one this spring. If not, if any man can figure out a way to put another gear in there that will allow us to run ahead again, he's the man that can."

"But that will take time, Ken."

"Not much, not if old Quillian will really put his back to the job. He's got a lathe, workshop, all kinds of stuff. By the way, when you buy groceries for the rest of the trip, will you get them from him? His prices are a bit steep, but that's the only way I can pay him for the work I want him to do for me."

Linda almost spurted out her mouthful of cocoa. She was vastly surprised.

"You mean he's a grocer, Ken? The way you spoke I thought he owned a dock-yard."

"I'm sorry, Linda." I was always forgetting how little she knew of this north country, so perfectly did she fit into it now. "Fur-trade, that's Quillian's business–having a tough time of it too. Bigger outfits making it hard for him, trying to squeeze him out. But he owns a boat of his own, loves boats, loves tinkering with them."

"And he'll take time off from his business to help you? And won't take pay for it?"

"Sure," I said.

It was that single word, the confidence I put into it, that delighted Linda.

"This is a wonderful country" she observed. "What was it you said once? 'Helpfulness and hospitality are the traditions of it–' something like that. Everybody helps everybody else. Everybody expects help when he gets stuck. Everybody offers pay when helped. Everybody refuses pay when helping. 'Pass it on' they say, like Jake and Izor yesterday. Tell me, Ken, what do you do when you get to the end of the season and tote up help given and help received and find you've got a debit balance and can't find anyone to pass help on to, to make the account square again? Doesn't your conscience bother you then?"

Half-playfully she asked the question, a mischievous twinkle in her blue eyes. Half-playful I answered it.

"That need never happen" I said. "There's always the Indians. I've never met one yet who wasn't urgently in need of help of some kind."

And even as I spoke the mouth of the River Between Two Mountains appeared around the point ahead, with natives' teepees on its shores. I turned the *Lady*'s wheel and pointed her nose toward them.

It was a small camp–three teepees, a tent, numerous dogs, four stages of fish hanging on sticks thrust through their tails, a moosehide stretched on a frame over a smoky fire, half a dozen fishnets curving in the eddy below the outlet, some of their floats violently moving. The Indians were doing what Indians should be doing at that time of year–preparing food and clothing for the winter. The dogs paid us a vociferous welcome, but the humans visible gave us little attention. A few ragged children playing on the beach lined up to watch us pull in, their small legs pathetically straight, wrinkled cotton stocking at various elevations about them. The *Lady*'s nose grounded gravel; Charley, rubbing the sleep out of his eyes, jumped ashore with the line, and almost immediately the children were gone, scuttling separately into the tents. One man stuck his head out of a tent flap, yawned, spat, grunted something to others behind him, then withdrew his head. An old lady squatting on the moose-hide went on scraping the hairs from it with a piece of bone, her round hunched back towards us. She was an immense fat old thing voluminously wrapped around with black skirts and black shawl.

Charley tied up, took the grub-box ashore, and started a little fire. Linda and I walked up to the biggest teepee. I knocked my knuckles on its nearest pole, but got no answer. I pulled the flaps aside and entered, closely followed by Linda.

There was a ring of about a dozen swarthy, lump-cheeked people lying, seated, or squatted on bedding close under the canvas walls, mostly full-grown men, a pack of cards distributed among them. A thin young woman with a persistent cough tended the central fire and a pot over it from which fish-heads protruded. She was something bothered by a squalling year-old baby which she held to her, soothing him occasionally by feeling about in the stew with a spoon till she found a fish's eye to pop into his mouth. That stopped the squalling.

I squatted on my heels.

"That girl Celestine Legentilhomme, go Wrigley have baby" I said, "her man here?"

From the opposite wall a grunt answered me. A hawk-faced lad seated there showed a faint glimmer of interest. I addressed myself to him.

"Your wife pretty bad sick" I said. "Savvy? Celestine bad sick. She go Simpson hospital. She go already by plane. Fly. Celestine fly Simpson. Savvy?"

And to aid comprehension I swept one hand in a slow arc oven my head, then put my thumbs against my shoulders and flapped my fingers up and down.

The man nodded.

"This woman"–I turned and pointed to Linda half-kneeling behind me– "she give Celestine her place on plane Wrigley airport. Give ticket, pay money, savvy? for nothing. Him sick, that's why."

Again young Hawk-face grunted. That was all the thanks Linda was likely to receive. Probably it was all she wanted, but I had hoped that she might get a pair of beaded moccasins offered to her.

"I go Simpson tomorrow" I said. "You got something send your wife? Message–writing?" And I pretended to scribble on my left hand with my right.

The man shook his head. One of his companions spoke, addressing another.

"Raise it two bits" he said.

I turned to Linda.

"I guess that's all. Let's get out into the fresh air."

"You forgot to tell him about the baby, Ken."

"Oh yes, the baby." I raised my voice again. "Your wife have baby, Wrigley–boy. (It was a boy, wasn't it, Linda?" "Yes.") I didn't see any way to break it gently. "That baby die" I said.

The man grunted his understanding and reached for two cards that had just been dealt into the space between his knees.

I raised the flap behind me and followed Linda into the sunshine. The fat old lady was still squatting on her moose-hide, still patiently scraping. She had removed the hair from possibly one more square inch since we had seen her last. Heads peeping out of other tents withdrew like Jacks-in-boxes as they felt our glances upon them.

Charley had the porridge already boiling.

"Not a very prepossessing people" Linda said a few minutes later. "Sugar, please."

"After you with the milk if you don't mind, Ken" said Charley. "What beats me is all the blasted filthy clothes they wear, like that guy I seen in the papers once they got him in hospital and they bathed him for three days before they discovered he had a suit of underwear on. Modess too, modess as ole hell. You ever go swimming with any them neestows, Ken? Men, I mean."

I helped myself to more porridge.

"They weren't always like that" I said. "According to Mackenzie when he came down here in 1789, they weren't modest at all–used to cover every part of the body except those parts which we consider

112

it most essential to cover. Most decent, I mean."

"You don't say" Linda exclaimed, and showed her modernity by asking for more details, which I unfortunately couldn't supply, Mackenzie's journals being very unsatisfactory in some places.

So we had ourselves a pleasant little meal on the beach, discussing our neighbours as we ate. About half an hour it took us: then we went concertedly to work, Linda packing the grub-boxes, Charley hauling in the lines, I pouring gasoline from one tank to another.

At the first pop out of the engine the flaps of the big teepee opened and young Hawk-face walked out. He carried a small greasy duffle bag in one hand, and had his best moccasins on. He stepped straight to the boat and sprang without hesitation onto her bow.

"Shoo!" said Charley. "I don't need any help push'n off."

The Indian paid no attention to him. He pigeon-toed straight aft along the gunnel, and after a moment's inspection of our accommodation, dropped his bag under the canvas shelter, and himself followed it.

Linda and the grub-box, I and the fourteen-inch Stillson, arrived at the same spot together. The Indian was already seated on the deck, his back comfortable against Charley's suitcase, his feet comfortable on my bedroll. He stopped rolling a cigarette to look up at me, showing very white teeth in a comradely grin.

"You go Simpson?" he asked.

"Yes. But—"

"I go too." He licked the cigarette paper and seemed to be waiting for somebody to offer him a match.

If it hadn't been for Linda, he wouldn't have got away with that. Her eyes were moving up and down, from him to me. She was smiling, much amused.

"You got some grub?" I asked. "Moosemeat? bannock? Something *meetsoo*?"

He shook his head.

"No grub."

"Get some."

He started to rise, slowly, not exactly offended, but certainly disappointed in us.

Linda touched my arm.

"We've got lots, Ken."

"Never mind" I said. "C'rrehh, C'rrehh."

He sat down again.

"You got dishes?" I asked. "Plate? Cup? Spoon?" I started to make appropriate gestures, then stopped, seeing that he was looking with interest at the porridge pot Linda had just set down nearby.

"Don't bother him" said Linda. "Poor man, his wife is dying, and he's on his way to see her."

At that moment Hawk-face rose slowly of his own volition and addressed a long gabble of epiglottis-bouncers to the old lady on the moosehide. She stopped her work to listen to him, grunted, slid to the ground, and waddled into the big teepee. In less than a minute she reappeared, carrying a small bundle done up in a stained flour-sack.

She walked straight to the boat and lifted the bundle for Charley to take it from her hands. Charley, standing on the bows with a push-pole ready, managed that well enough, but wasn't prepared for what came next. She came. With surprising agility, she hoisted herself right up on to the deck, sending the *Lady*'s nose grinding into the gravel.

The Indian lad smiled at me.

"That my mudder-in-law" he said.

"Send her ashore."

"Me no boss, that woman, me."

"Well, damn it, I am here–" but again Linda stopped me.

"That makes her Celestine's mother," she said.

"But where's everybody going to sleep?" I asked. "And who's going to feed em all" You don't know these people, Linda. Eat?–a four pound tin of jam to a meal, that's their style, when somebody else is paying for it. And lice–they've got special permission from the priests to eat them on Fridays." I went one into numerous details and difficulties, and I suppose I carried on much too long. All the time I argued with Linda the old lady was also gabbling, directing a long stream of noise ashore, waving her arms about in a way that had Charley jumping to keep from being pushed overboard.

I stopped at last to listen to her. I could make out only a word or so here and there–"*cuzz-e-cal*, come here", "*deerie-eeschew*, I'll take that", and "*Besainchew*, give it to me." The beach was swarming with people now, men and women trotting in and out of the teepees in the sort of dignifiedly hurried way they have at times, dogs barking at the end of chains, children forming a line near the bows.

I love children–some of them.

114

"Who are those kids?" I asked."

The Indian lad showed his gleaming teeth again.

"That my brudder. That my sister his boy. That one this side my wife his cousin. That–"

I didn't wait to hear any more. Bundles were coming out of the teepees now, dogs being untied and led towards us, the children gathering in big-eyed bunches just out of reach of Charley's push-pole.

"Shove off!" I shouted.

"Remember the traditions, Ken" Linda said, enjoying it all immensely

We were soon into the safety of deep water, soon pointed upstream. On the beach behind us the Indians stared a while, then began leading their dogs back to the chain-posts, carrying their bundles inside the tents. In the waist under the shelter-canvas Hawk-face rolled himself in my sleeping bag and went to sleep.

On the bow-deck the old lady squatted with shoulders sagging, fat legs unimaginably contorted under the cone of her black skirts, lank black hair blowing in the wind of our passage, her weight so much to one side that Charley had to move a full gas-barrel two feet to port before he could balance the boat. In the pilot-house Linda, chuckling often, tore the last page from my log-book, ruled it into parallel columns of "Help Given" and "Help Received", and started making entries. She allowed me two points for the new figure-head we carried.

About noon that day we arrived within sight of the lower tip of McGern Island, and I didn't know which way to go. Lunky Thorvalt-sen, who knew as much about the river as any man, had marked the steam-boat channel on my charts, but this particular part of them had got involved in some misadventures since and was no longer legible. It had apparently fallen on the deck at some time and been tramped on by Charley in muddy boots. In places Lunky's notes were visible and ominous: "Rock", "Big Rock," "Rocks all along here–keep well out" the notes said, but the fine arrows originally pointing to the spots in which these dangers lay were quite obliterated.

I called Hawk-face aft, taking a certain pleasure in waking him.

"Joe, you know river here?"

"Sure, I know river, me."

"Which side we go, this island?"

I showed him the chart. He examined it with great interest, peered at it a long time, finally spoke.

"This side that side more quick. My fadder that side big rock camp-it two years. Fast. Shoot moose. No?"

"No" I said.

"I go he come. Two day go bush. Big rock, yes, big, big rock." His eyes opened wide to express greatness, his hands enlarged greatness further yet, outlining something that had the shape of an apple dumpling. "Savvy?"

"Savvy" I said.

"This side that side more quick" he repeated. He stabbed violently at the paper with one dirt-grimed finger. "Big, big, big, you savvy?"

"You bet" I said. "Big. Look Joe, you go up on the bow and show me which way to go. Savvy?"

"Sure" he said, showed his white teeth again, and immediately trotted up to the bows.

The result of all that was that about half an hour later we nosed around a small island that looked too close to shore for my liking, nosed into a channel that I didn't like the look of at all, and heard a sound which I likes less yet–the barking of dogs.

There was a muddy looking tent erected under a rock on the beach, a round old rock shaped something like a dumpling, a big rock, big, big, big. An Indian stood beside it, and he was quite big too.

The boy jumped over his mother-in-law's skirts, pigeon-toed aft along the gunnel again, and once more favoured us with his white-toothed smile.

"My fadder" he said simply. "Tank you."

Up on the bows the fat old bundle of skirts began directing her flow of gabble shorewards, leaning so far to one side that Charley, Linda, and I all had to play sardines against the port wall of the pilot-house.

If it had been just the old man I wouldn't have minded. Jean-Baptiste Legentilhomme was a good-looking old boy, in a proudly cruel sort of way, with even more hawk in his nose than in his son's, and had vast quantities of that dignity some of the old-timer natives have–a dignity which so far as I know is not to be seen anywhere else on earth, based not so much on the individual's sense of his own worth as on his sense of the worth of any individual anywhere. "You're a man" his eyes seemed to say, "and I am a man too. Nothing else counts." And no amount of fleas and wide-spaced spitting could detract one jot from the direct gaze of those eyes.

It was his relatives, the boy's relative's, the mother-in-law's innumerable cousins, whom I objected to. It seemed incredible that one small mud-coloured tent could hold half a dozen people, that that little teepee six miles further up the river could hold three, that the decrepit log cabin around the next bend could shelter eight. We took them all aboard: after the first five or so it seemed pointless to refuse the rest.

"Aw, let em come" said Charley, "we'll have to scrub every damn plank in her when we get to Simpson anyways."

Once admitted to our company they took a lot for granted. Naturally they couldn't read the "Private" sign Charley had stuck up in front of the little sleeping-cubby he and I had built in the bows for Linda; but I did manage to get some of her gear safely stowed before they overflowed into it and began using her fingernail polish. I was more worried by the canoes they tied astern without telling me–they swamped in our wash, all but drowning the dogs chained in them. We took the canoes aboard then, slinging them cross-wise on the bow deck about the old lady who apparently considered this a sight-seeing excursion and refused to budge from her priority spot for anyone. We took the dogs aboard too, tying them down to six inches of free chain, whenever possible trying to arrange them with their after-ends hanging overboard.

We chased the whole gang ashore when we tied up that night, of course. I had a notion to pull out in the morning before any of them were awake, and might have done so too, but Linda wouldn't let me.

"Remember the traditions of the North" she said, and waved the ledger she had been keeping before my eyes. It was her opinion that by the time we reached Simpson I would have earned in advance every ounce of help I wanted to receive there.

Scratching myself vigorously, I agreed wholeheartedly with her. Lunky, Jake, Izor, and every other man in the North who had ever turned his hand in my favour–they were all repaid in full now. If I hadn't have happened to stand too close to old Legentilhomme at some time during the day, I think I might have been quite content

117

with the situation. I had never felt one half so virtuous in my life before– nor one quarter so lousy.

Sir Alexander Mackenzie, when he first visited the river named after him, noted with some interest the peculiarity of its water for some miles below the point on which Simpson now stands. He cannot have gazed at it with more interest than Charley and I did as we approached the settlement. Along the right bank flowed the clean, clear water fresh from Great Slave Lake. Along the left bank flowed the dirty flood water fresh from the Liard River. It was up the Liard that we were determined to travel, and we were greatly pleased to observe that for this time of the year the water that it contributed to the Mackenzie was unusually dirty. That could only mean that the Liard was running unusually high.

Our theories were confirmed as soon as we stepped ashore.

"Yeh, she's way up for this time of the year" said one Simpsonian. "If you don't draw over four foot, you'll make the rapids easy." That was excellent news: the *Lady* drew about two foot six.

"But you'll have to hurry" said a second, "for she's due to start dropping any day soon."

"My God! looka the neestows pouring outa that little scow" said a third. "My God! there's another one. My God! where'd you fellows keep them all? My God!"

That last invocation to the deity was produced by Linda's appearing in the pilot-house doorway, after which number three maintained an enraptured silence.

I hurried up to see old Quillian, and after the usual exchanges about the weather and my beard, got down to business.

"Find a left-hand prop for me yet, Quillian?"

He shook his head. "None in the country."

"What do you think about running her in reverse with a right-hander? Do her gears any harm?"

He raised his thin eyebrows. "You going all the way up the Liard?"

"Yes."

His eyebrows drew together in a frown. "You'd never make it runnin' that way" he said.

I knew he was right. The *Lady*'s gears had been getting noticeably noisy the last few miles. I put my problem before him, asked if he could help me. He shut up his big ledgers, cleared a place on the counter, began to draw sketches. This sort of thing was his hobby and his delight; the shelves of goods around him, the account books, the fur-price lists, were no more than a means of livelihood and a source of headaches. The few customers that dropped in he served and dismissed as quickly as he could.

Only once did he briefly lose interest in the discussion we were having. He looked up, peered out a side window, frowned.

"Be damned if that ginkus walking boi didn't look loike ould Buchess Leyuntiyum" he remarked. "Just got a glimpse of him out of the tail of me oye. Can't be him."

"One of my own men, ould Buchees" he explained. "That's what I call the beggar anyway. You've got your own bunch of Indians, so you call them, and so they swear by the holy mither they are. But you know how it is, Ken, you used to be a fur-trader yourself one time. Don't give them too much debt, or you'll never see their ugly faces in your store again. Don't give them too little, or they'll start dickering with somebody else for sure. Worry, worry, worry. The ounly time a trader knows any peace is when his Indians are off in the bush."

"I know" I said, and "Now, about that cog-wheel you were speaking of"–I said". It seemed to me like an excellent time to change the subject, quick. I was being seized of a premonition.

"Well" said old Quillian, "Oi can't really say till I take a look at her myself. Oi tell you, you go down and start tearing her apart, and Oi'll lock up and join you as soon as I can. We'll troi to get you going again first thing tomorra morning."

And just at that moment, of course, in walked hawk-nose Joe and Linda. Quillian stared first at one, then at the other, as if unable to believe his eyes about either. Linda had done some work on her face since I saw her last, and was looking very pretty indeed. She looked quite intelligent too; but she wasn't; not one item of the sign-language I hastily sent her way had any effect at all. She even had the nerve to say afterwards that she thought I was just itching badly again.

She walked right up to me with a little list she had made.

"Thought I'd find you here, Ken" she said brightly. "Look, do you think I ought to get more pork and beans, or will thirty-six tins be enough? If you'll just check the list, I'll get the stuff, and Joe here says he'll carry it down to the boat for us at once. Old Baptiste the Gentleman is coming to help us too, as soon as he's been to see the

119

girl in the hospital. They're nice, really nice, all of them, all so anxious to do something to repay us for bringing them upriver."

The effect of those words had hardly ceased bouncing from eye to eye in the room before the fat old mother-in-law waddled through the door, directing a long stream of gabble at the multitude that surged behind her. One after another they came shuffling in then, smiling at Linda and me as at past comrades-in-arms, dignifiedly going up to shake hands with old Quillian, spitting in the general direction of the tomato can by the door, hoisting their behinds on the counter, avidly eyeing the shelves which he had confidently stocked with goods as soon as he had got rid of them, the whole nineteen of them, three weeks before.

We left Fort Simpson with strong determinations, fair auspices, and gloomy predictions.

"It's royal weather for this time of the year" said Thurber, the Indian agent. "But it might change overnight. In '39 there was two feet of snow and the ice was running in the river on this date. If you can get up the Chutes you'll be all right. Keep to the left most of the way."

"She's a fast boat, Oi'll say that for her" said Quillian. "That engine'll take you over the Chutes if you ever get that far, but you won't; you'll stick on the Beaver Dam for sure and all. Keep to the right most of the way, then cross over."

"Hope the water ain't cold for swimming" said Cherhill, the woodcutter. "Robertson, when he tried it in '42 same time o' year, he went side-wise down the rapids thirteen times before he guv up. Water was higher then, too. You fellows better keep to the middle channel all the way."

"How come sidewise?" Charley asked, though he should have known better.

"Fourteen times, that's what Oi heard" said Quillian.

"Fifteen, Quill, fifteen times" said Thurber, "remember how Robbie used to tick them off on his fingers when he was telling the story?"

"Sure, and he had one finger missing on his left hand" Cherhill reminded us all. "One finger off right here, you don't wanna forget that, Jack. Thirteen, see? One, two, three, and you end up next the missing one."

"How come?" Charley asked again.

"Aw, he was splittin' kindlin', and one of kids run up from behint–"

"I don't mean that," said Charley. "I mean how come sidewise?"

"Hell, you otta know. You get up so far, you see, then your rudders rub on the ledge, and your bow swings, and down you come, sidewise. Thirteen times."

"Fifteen, Al. Four on the Beaver Dam, two on the Chutes, three–"

"Fowrteen, Peter. Foive on the Baver Dam, and none on the Chutes. Nobody's come soidewise down the Chutes and lived to tell the tale of it, niver."

"Thirteen, Mike. Look, double this here finger down, and start here. One... two... three... See?"

"Fowrteen, Al..."

"Fifteen, Mike.... "

"Thirteen, I tell ye, dammit, look.... "

They were still arguing when we pushed the *Lady*'s nose out into the stream and gunned the eager motor. They were probably still arguing, a knot of vehement little figures black on the snow-covered beach behind us, when we swung to starboard under Gros Cap, left behind us the familiar Mackenzie, which had given us adventures enough to satisfy any reasonable cravings already, and entered into the still more difficult waters of the Liard. It seems odd now to think of that ridiculous argument, to recall that none of that three told none of our three that what we proposed to do was madness at that time of year, that we were in fact fools to try it. I suppose they thought we knew that already. I suppose also that in our hearts, we did.

Five days later the *Lady Greenbelly* ploughed from shore to shore, back and forth across the muddy stream of the Liard River, seeking deeper water. She had never run better, never run more quietly, never leaped forward more willingly when her gear lever was shifted into the "ahead" position, thanks to Quillian's mechanical ingenuity. And never had I had less opportunity to make the most of the power she offered me. Again and again Charley, up on the bows with a sounding pole, suddenly shook his head, hastily pointed this way or that; again and again I swing the wheel hurriedly over, throttled down, listened to rocks grinding slowly under the stern. I had much to curse about that morning; and I did.

Charley threw his pole down on the deck and came aft.

"Looks okay for a ways" he said, "but it won't last. God, Ken, see that bar stickin' up there? I was lookin' at this spot from up'n the bank day after we come in, and Hell! there wasn't even shallow water there then."

I nodded. "Yes, she's gone down at least two feet in the last four days."

"The last four days." Charley repeated the words as if he wanted to be sick over them. Then he sighed. "Can't blame old Quillian, I guess. Business is business an' he hadda get them neestows away 'fore he could tend to us."

"Of course," I agreed. "He's a better fur-trader than ever I was, too. He told me this morning old Legentilhomme didn't get into him for more than another hundred dollars before he finally packed him off. And the whole lot chased back to the bush in four days–that's good going, Charley."

Charley sighed again. "Them four days–if it hadn't been for them, Ken, I think we might have had a chance to make them rapids ahead. Now–" He broke off, shrugged his shoulders, and went forward to his sounding pole again.

Linda, gazing through the pilot-house windows, had taken no part in this conversation. I turned to her.

"Linda, what do you think of the traditions of the country now?"

"There's only one word for them" she answered. She smiled a little before she told me what it was, as disappointed as we were, but amused too. She cupped one hand about her mouth, and, careful not to stand too close to me, whispered into my ear.

"They're lousy" she said.

122

Chapter 13

The *Lady* Wins the Booby-Prize

They say the rapids of the Liard River begin about forty miles above its mouth, that they make treacherous navigation for another twelve miles or so, and that from there on the remaining two hundred and fifty miles to Nelson Forks are fair going. Estimates vary because estimators vary, because also the rapids themselves vary a little from year to year, and more from season to season. They grow in fury and in length all through the summer, as the water level drops. Navigation of them in any large scale is considered impractical after the first of August, impossible after the end of September. So men say: I can tell only what I know from my own experience.

You strike your first fast water opposite the bottom tip of a large island about fifteen miles up. Whether you call that rapids or not depends on your definition of rapids, and probably on how much trouble you have in climbing it. The channel lies close outside an immense boulder sunk in the bed of the stream with a four-foot high V of wave lashing out from it. I call that rapids. Right there would have been a good place to give up and turn back, as others have done before us. We made it on the third try.

The next twenty miles are fairly good going. There's a definite channel winding from bank to bank in the normal manner, four feet deep at a minimum and fairly easy to see if you can read water at all. As far as I can remember there's half a dozen small rapids–or riffles if you like–in this part, three long gravel bars, and one place where if you don't know the river you are almost certain to steer into a false channel. The map shows two small islands also, but during the day we spent making this twenty miles it was snowing too hard for us to see them. It was the tenth of October.

That's the first thirty-five miles. Add two more tumultuous riffles, with big rocks in them and some sort of a channel about a hundred yards off the left shore, and you reach the Beaver Dam. There's no doubt about that–that's rapids, though a purist might object that it is properly a cascade, and would have been right a few years ago. Old rivermen say that there used to be a solid ledge of limestone stretching across the river there, curved slightly, just as a beaver dam would be, and just as flat on top. That single four-foot drop in those days rendered the whole Liard unnavigable any time after midsummer. In recent years, however, some agency–explosives used by the American Army, some men say, grinding spring ice, others insist–has worn part of the ledge away a quarter mile out from the left shore, reducing the straight drop to an inclined one about twenty feet long. Admittedly the American Army did much scenery-changing in these parts during '43 and '44, but I think myself that it was ice that made the difference. You can see long scratches on the limestone not three feet under the sliding surface as you creep up against the current and the rubbing of your rudders. You don't have time to see them as you slide downstream again. Four time I saw them: three times I didn't have time.

Above the Beaver Dam you turn sharp to port and cut square across to the right shore. What looked like one rapids ahead of you then fingers out to two. You take the lower of these about fifteen yards out, either side of a big rock sticking out of the water. I don't remember which is the better side, which we tried first, which enabled us to grind through at last. The next rapids you take as close to shore as you dare, inside another big boulder. If you haven't got quite power enough to stem the current there you can put a man ashore and have him haul your port gunnel along as you slide by. Charley proved very useful at that sort of work.

Immediately after that you turn sharp to starboard and cut a mile across river to the left bank again. You head straight for a high cliff rising almost sheer from the water and making a distinctive point in the river valley. The Chute Rapids are the next, the worst in the river, men say, and the only passage up them lies in the chute from which they take their name, close under that high cliff.

Sneaking close up under the cliff, but not too close till the point begins to round out before you, you can climb possibly one foot of the drop before you get into difficulties. It's a good idea then to poke your bows into shore, gather together a half ton of rocks to tie your line to, and get off and look around. That's my advice: but, brother, if you've managed to get that far, when you hear the Chute's roaring in your ears, and feel its fury twisting at your helm, you won't need to be told.

Although it was still an hour to dark, we made camp right away. We sawed into our last loaf of Simpson bread, opened our last tin of jam, and ate heartily, too excited to cook ourselves a proper meal. This, we all knew, was IT, though none of us said a word about it.

"Thirteen" Charley said as we neared the end of our repast.

"Fourteen" said Linda, "if you count the time we went sideways down the Sans Sault, long ago. Ages ago, it seems."

"Oh yeh, fourteen for us, shore, count'n that one, though we shouldn't, really" Charley agreed. "But what I'm tryna figure is how many times Robertson did it. Which finger was it he had cut off, Ken? Didya notice which one they said?"

"It doesn't matter" I said. "You hold any finger down with your thumb, any finger at all, see, like this, and you count–No, no, you don't not count the thumb just because it's holding down one of your fingers–Look, Charley, that's all wrong; start with the thumb and –"

Linda watched us awhile, then rose from the fire and ambled slowly along the beach, holding a slice of bread and jam with the shape of her lower jaw already chomped out of it. On the narrow ledge between high cliff and fast water she idly picked up a loose slab of flat limestone. She looked at it briefly, then came hurrying back.

"Look, Ken. Charley, look. Fossils!"

The previously unexposed underside of the rock was covered with little twigs, little bundles of something that looked like acorns and were stone now, minute tracks of minute insects that had crawled among twigs and acorns ages ago. Soon Charley and I were scrambling up and down the face of the cliff, finding similar remains of ancient life at every level. We gathered dozens of specimens around the fire, examined them, compared them, announced our finds with childish shouts of glee.

125

Then wandering down the beach we discovered the suckers. In a small bay just below the point we found them. They lay almost still in the water, greyish indistinct objects blending with the rocks to which their obscene mouths held them. A gently waving fin betrayed one to Charley's keen eyes. He waved his arm over the spot. Instantly then they were gone, all those shadowy shapes. One moment they were there, the next they weren't. Then, as suddenly, they were there again. Going and coming, we could not see them. We laughed, waved our arms, said "Shoo!", said "Come fish' come fish; nice fish", and laughed again.

We tried to catch them.

"No damn good to eat" said Charley. "Taste like sulphur, suckers."

Yet he was the first to flatten himself stealthily on the lowest, water-licked ledge, to poise and plunge his arm, to withdraw it empty of hand–a two hundred pound, thirty-five year old man in ragged paint-smeared overalls, bearded, much in need of a haircut, and acting like a child of ten. Linda and I waited our turns eagerly, took them when they came gleefully, and had no better luck than he.

We warmed pork and beans, ate them in the pink light of the fire, and went to our separate sleeping robes without one word said about the Chute that we had traveled arduously to reach and found more furious than anything we had imagined when we did reach it. Charley said later that we were all slap-happy, punch-drunk. Perhaps he was right, but I think myself that we were each of us waiting for another to say that we were obviously beaten now, that we might just as well give up and turn back. But none of us said so: we talked of fish and fossils instead.

The next morning, looking out my pilot-house window with my head turned to port, I had a good view of the Chute Rapids. In the distance all was a turmoil of leaping water and big stones black with the spray upon them; but nearer, close to port, through the green sheen of racing water I could see the underlying formation of limestone which caused the rapids. It was a series of vast steps like the steps leading from some great public building of old, partly in ruins, with many unevennesses in them, many fissures. In some of these fissures boulders were wedged, granite from far upriver, limestone from nearby–the broken walls and columns from the broken building.

About these boulders the water played enormously, stridently hissing. Thus close by, it was the hissing you heard, a hissing that rose above the roar that struck your ears as you came upriver towards the rapids. Yet if you put your mind to it, you could hear the roaring still, booming and surging in the background of all the noise about you, ominous, causing your blood to race.

We had achieved a perfect balance of forces half-way up the chute, the throbbing motor thrusting full blast one way, the hissing water thrusting full blast the other. Along the outer edge of the chute close to the broken rim of the steps an underwater eddy had helped us so far, pushing with the engine. So we moved quite rapidly at first, Charley getting "no bottom" on his pole all the way. Then he frantically signaled "two feet", and as I turned the nose shoreward to avoid the obstruction that caused the eddy, we stopped moving up. For ten minutes we simply hung there, looking the situation over.

We were alone on the boat that first time, Charley and I. The *Lady*, for all my pride in her, was no more than an open scow after all, about thirty feet long, narrow and low. One big wave catching her right would swamp her all in a second. So on that first attempt I had insisted on Linda staying ashore.

I should have worried about my boat during those days. I was ruining her. Four times already since we left Simpson we had had to take the rudders off and straighten them. The propeller I had not seen, but many times I had heard gravel and rock pinging against it. Worse than that, her flat wooden bottom had endured five days of almost steady grinding and bumping on hard rocks. I had big plans for the *Lady* for the next season. I wanted to get her at or near Fort Nelson that fall, I said, so that I would be in a favourable position to start the following spring's freighting. But the way this trip was going I would have lost more than I gained by the time I got her there. If I had been a practical businessman I should have turned back several days before.

But instead of worrying about the boat, I was worrying about Linda. She was as much of a volunteer aboard as Charley even if she had practically forced herself on us back at the Rampart Rapids three weeks before. Yet I worried about her much, about Charley not at all. She was a woman, a weaker creature, and had no part in this business at all. I had no right to risk her life in this manner.

I turned my head to look to starboard. Under the great cliff she sat on a narrow ledge of rock, primeval solid vast immobility towering immense behind and above her, angry water rushing violently past her feet. She didn't worry about herself, about danger, about loss of herself or her possessions. Her only worry stemmed from the fact that with all our irregularity of diet, hard work, and consequently large appetites, she had apparently been putting on weight ever since she had joined us. Quillian's scales at Simpson had given her a shock. Rapids didn't; danger never seemed to distress her at all.

She was getting bored now, weary of watching this futile attempt to climb the chute under our own power. She sat on the ledge with her elbows on her knees, one thumb pointing upstream, her face wearing the perkily diffident expression common to hitch-hikers. When she saw that I was looking at her, she stuck out her tongue at me. She wasn't at all pleased to be left there on the shore.

I eased the motor and let the *Lady* drop back to her stopping place. I had no intention of trying it again. We were licked.

"What now?"

"Damned if I know."

"What about lines, tracking her up?"

"Shore. Mebbee. Try it anyway."

That was Linda and Charley talking. I, captain and owner of the boat, never got a word in.

Charley and I yoked ourselves to a long line ashore, and pulled till our very intestines seemed stretched out as long as the rope and in greater danger of breaking. Charley didn't put it quite that way. With Linda at the wheel, the life-belt around her neck and one arm through it, we got the *Lady* about a quarter of the way up the Chute in that manner, then had to drop back again. We stopped to have lunch.

"What now?"

"Let's try block and tackle."

"Will that work?"

"Let's try it."

Again I had no say.

We used treble blocks and about four hundred feet of rope. Charley and I knocked the peak out of our canvas shelter, put our feet against the after end of the bow deck, and pulled till we couldn't open our fingers fast enough to play the Death March. We had the nose up to the top of the chute before the line fouled on a sharp edge of limestone, and instantly parted.

"Couldna've got her any further anyways" said Charley then, rolling a cigarette.

"No", I agreed. "We couldn't. Any more suggestions?"

"Only thing left is to build a winch."

"Any winch we could build, there wouldn't be room to work it on our bows."

"Build it ashore then. Build a capstan, and haul the boat up to it." That was Linda, of course, her eyes shining, her soul actually delighted, I do believe, because we had not succeeded yet and had more opportunities for fun and games ahead of us. For her sake, I hope she has grandchildren sometime, to listen to the tales she'll be able to tell them.

"A lot of work" I said, "if we can do it at all, which I doubt. Let's vote on it."

The vote was unanimous, my own hand coming up last of all.

It took the rest of that day and all the next to build the capstan. We scoured the beach two miles each way to find suitable planks from the flotsam scattered along shore. We cut holes in the planks with the hatchet, burnt them round and true with heated irons. We felled a dead spruce on the heights two hundred feet above the river, rolled a six foot section of it down a sand-slide in the cliff, fitted it to the holes, notched and fluted it for the rope, and burnt a great hole in it to put the bar through. We moved ton upon ton of rock to anchor the winch down when it was completed at last. We ate twenty-two tins of pork and beans while we were doing the job, not because we particularly liked pork and beans, but because that was about all the food we had left.

Then one fine cold morning Charley took the wheel, I walked the bar around in a twenty-foot circle cleared of fossils for the purpose, Linda kept the rope taut as it came off the drum. It was touch and go all the way. Once we had to leave Charley hanging at the end of the rope for twenty minutes while we heaped more rocks around the winch. Once Charley had to leave the wheel ten minutes while he wrapped his sleeping robe around the rope where it chafed on the bows.

129

Then, suddenly, the struggle was over. The line came in easily, faster than I could turn it up. The *Lady* moved on her own power into the calm bay above the chutes.

Aboard, Charley pretended that the sounding pole stuck in its socket beside the pilot-house was a banana-tree, and himself a monkey. Ashore, Linda let the rope slip from her hands with a dazed expression, then suddenly threw her arms around my neck, and, for the first and only time in our association, kissed me, raising one heel in the air behind her. When Charley joined us, she kissed him too.

They say that the worst is over once you've passed the Chutes. The rapids continue for a few miles, but are not bad. So they say: I can tell only what I know. You start to angle slowly towards the other shore soon after you leave the Chutes, heading for another high cliff on the opposite side which makes the next point in the valley. There's no definite channel that I could find, but there is a wide run where the water would give three feet if it wasn't for the big boulders lying on the bottom.

The water is fast, but not fast enough to show up those boulders plainly. I put Charley and Linda both on the bows, sounding and watching continually, one to the port and one to starboard. For all their care, we hit often. Sometimes we were then able to keep going till we had bumped a way over; sometimes we had to let the boat swing till the current washed us off.

Charley was happy. Every time we passed sidewise over even the smallest riffle he stuck one finger hopefully into the air, hopefully looked at Linda. She was happy too; smiling, she shook her head at him; no, you really couldn't add that one to the thirteen if you wanted to be honest about it. Charley would look to right or left then till he spotted a true rapids somewhere and cheerfully wave for me to steer towards it. If we were going to beat Robertson's record we'd have to do it soon, before we ran out of rapids altogether.

As often, the best water lay near the biggest boulders in the stream. Halfway to the point we passed between two immense ones, big as railway locomotives, then struck hard on a small one between them. I knew we were going to hit. Charley and Linda had both signaled this rock to me, but neither of them had found a way around it. I bore down on the throttle, felt the bow strike and lift, felt the *Lady* heave again as she rubbed on the rock amidship, felt it grind slowly astern, slowly and more slowly, till it stopped.

I looked about then. We had to swing one way or the other to get off, would go sidewise a while then, would almost inevitably drift sidewise into one or other of those giant boulders astern. The question was, which one? We had noticed when making tally of our previous mishaps that it had so happened that we had always swing to the right when making our sidewise passages down rapids. Now that the danger was over I became conscientious about my boat and decided that in this case I would swing to port, to give the starboard chine a rest.

I turned the wheel, the bows swing, slowly at first, then rapidly, water poled up alongside, the rock ground slowly thwartwise under the engine. I tried to straighten out before we hit the big rock, but couldn't make it. We hit just aft of amidship, then began to swing at once under the superior pressure of the water against the bows. The water was fast enough to produce that effect immediately, fast enough also to tilt us far over to port before we slid free.

It was a minor incident in our experience. A mere trifle it seemed at first. Charley and Linda didn't even go down on their hands and knees to keep from being jostled off the bow-deck, and we weren't even free before Charley was hopefully sticking one finger into the air again. Linda shook her head: that was no decent try for the booby-prize.

At that moment the engine stopped. It gave a little cough, two resounding back-pops, then stopped dead. The ensuing silence was complete for a few seconds, till the ears picked up again the swish of water alongside, the gurgle of it passing around those two big rocks already fifty feet astern, and the great roar of the Chute rapids a mile below us.

I dashed into the engine room and pressed on the starter. I was still pressing it when Linda came rushing aft, ducked down the steps, and bent over beside me.

"Sounded like water in the gas, Ken. Charley's trying to ground her on a bar."

It *was* water in the gasoline. I understand now, but I didn't then. The tank under the pilot-house was an old forty-five gallon drum laid athwartship on its side with the outlet from the lower bung on the port side. While the *Lady* lay heeled to port against the big rock which I had wilfully chanced hitting in preference to the one on the

131

other side, water accumulated during many months below the bung had poured into the feedline. The sediment bulb was full of it now; so was the feedline; so was the carburetor; so, undoubtedly, was the engine.

Linda broke the line aft of the fuel-pump, let liquid pour into the bilge till rust-coloured water gave place to good red gasoline, then made the joint, choked the carburetor, opened the throttle, and pressed on the starter.

"Whirr! Whirr! Whirr!"

The metallic rattle, the hiss of air sobbing into the choke, momentarily drowned the noise of rocks scraping along the bottom beneath us and the increasing roar of the rapids below us.

Linda closed the throttle, opened the choke, pressed the starter again.

"Whirr! Whirr! Whirr!"

It was slower now: I'd worked the battery hard before she took charge.

She gave a little throttle, a little choke, tried again.

"Whirr! Whirr! Whirr!"

The metallic clanging ceased. The roar of the rapids drummed through the portholes, ebbing and rising as the boat swung slowly under the force of the current and Charley's desperate poling.

"It's no use, Ken. We'll have to clean the plugs–four at least, in firing order, to be sure."

She was remarkably calm. It was a pity the Spars, which had made so accomplished a mechanic of her, had never given her the chance for action that she expected of them. She would have medals to show.

"This one" she said, "and this–and this–and this."

We took them out, fumbling the wrenches, gave them a puff and a lick with a rag, put them back in again.

"Whirr! Whirr! Whirr!"

The engine started, Charley shouted, I said "We'd better get out of here", and we hit the first ledge on the Chute Rapids all in the same instant. I'm glad the engine started: it wasn't the least bit of use to us in what followed, and it quit again some few unknown minutes later; but just the same I am glad it started.

Charley at first had tried to push into a midstream shallows, but had seen them drift by us in what seemed an incredibly short time. He had then tried to push us to the nearest shore. As his hope of that failed, he had kept pushing in the same direction, hoping to drive us into the strong water bearing towards the Chute. He was almost successful in that objective. We hit, port side first, with the after end of the *Lady* actually overhanging the deep water of the Chute, the rest of her striking evenly against the boulders embedded in the top flight of steps.

Those boulders were solid there. They had resisted the force of vast weights of ice before this. They resisted the *Lady* now. Some of them stuck inches out of water. She couldn't slide over them. Neither could she stay where she was. A huge wall of water piling up against her starboard side was strongly urgent that she move.

She moved. She leaned to port, quickly at first, then slowly, slowly, till she reached a balance point–then quickly again, falling heavily on her port side. In that position she slid, jarred, and bumped down several steps till more projections stopped her.

Then she rolled again, much more quickly than before. She simply flipped over onto her gunnels and started to jar and slide down the steps again, bottom up.

Linda and I were in the pilot-house by then, and the pilot-house was completely under water, in the depths of the Chute. As Charley said later, things looked bad for a minute, though she was in a grand position for caulking the bottom seams. For his part, he was spraddled on the curve of the bow, with part of the push-pole in one hand. He never could remember how he got there or when that pole broke.

The upstream eddy which I had noticed running close to the steps in the Chute now took a part in our activities. The water pouring down the slope had quarter-rolled us twice, and tended to roll us again as soon as our sliding gunnels struck against yet more embedded boulders. But we had our widest part down now, and I don't think even that forceful current could have flipped us over again if the eddy in the Chute had not levered against the pilot-house in the opposite direction.

Linda and I weren't long in the water. Suddenly green daylight appeared in the rectangle of the doorway towards which we were struggling, then blue sky, with water curtaining down it from the roof–that roof incredibly over our heads again. It was a full half-roll this time, setting the *Lady* upright. Again wood ground on rocks, slipping, sliding, jarring; but the wood was bottom-planking now.

We struggled to our feet, looked through the pilot-house windows–only one pane broken–saw the engine room walls shattered below us, saw the hull full of water, saw our baggage floating in it, saw the canvas shelter fallen and humped over more of our belongings, saw Charley clambering up the port side to the bow deck, shaking the water out of his hair.

The after end struck, hard. The bow end, riding freely, swung down-stream. The water in the hull raced forward, ballooning out the canvas, pouring through the open peak, swooshing about Charley as he stood on the bow deck, carrying overboard nearly all of our possessions that were not already bobbing in the water below us. Only my canoe jammed under the canvas. Only Linda's sleeping robe did Charley manage to grab and hold on to of all the gear that swept around him. Our gas-barrels were gone, an empty one dancing in the waves far ahead of us, two full ones grinding and bumping down the steps after us.

It was perhaps lucky that we had left them behind when we rolled over. Their additional weight might have done for us when we ground off the last ledge and slipped out into the deep water below the chute. With a bare six inches of freeboard to spare, we poled slowly to the beach.

"Fourteen?" said Charley. "Hell, what's it matter? Robertson or nobody else never rolled plumb over in a rapids before."

"She'll run all right as soon as we dry the leads" said Linda, her teeth chattering now with cold and afterfright. "And, Ken, don't forget I still want some of those fossils to take home with me."

"You'll have them," said I, "but let me take the canoe and get after our gear before I do anything else. Fellows at Simpson, seeing that stuff floating by, they might think something unpleasant had happened to us."

So we talked, and so we acted, bailing out, starting a fire, gathering our possessions about us again, picking up the threads of life afresh; but not one of us said another word about trying the Chute a second time.

134

Chapter 14

The *Lady*'s Parting Shots

This should be Charley's story rather than mine, and I should like to hear him tell it. With his notion that the gods of the North were after me, he could make more sense of it than I can. To me, it just happened so; to him, there was a purpose behind it.

Charley didn't call them gods, of course. He balked at the paganism of naming any divinity without using a capital "G". The powers he spoke of he accordingly referred to simply as "they"; but he believed in "them" for all of that. I had defied "them", he said: I had vowed that I was going to take my boat from Aklavik to Fort Nelson in the fall of the year despite "them" and be damned to "them", and any sharp rap on the knuckles I got on the way, of which there had been plenty, was only evidence of the displeasure my presumption had caused "them". That made sense up to a point, up in fact to the point when "they" took and rolled Linda, him, myself, the *Lady*, and all our gear sidewise down the Chute Rapids in the Liard River. After that it didn't make sense; for at that point I gave up, I called it quits, I sought nothing but to salvage as much of the wreckage as I could, to store it for another attempt in another year, and to flee the country by the quickest means available. So, I told Charley, "they" ought to leave me alone now, and I would take it as a favour if he would stop harping on the subject himself. And though I laughed, I remember toying with the thought that these hostile gods he would not name might actually bless me in my going; for after all it was not a bad fight I had put up against "them", and it would be gentlemanly of them not to kick me now that I was down.

That thought was too generous. "They" took another crack at me before I so much as left the scene of the accident, right on the beach below the rapids that had finally defeated us. This "they" of Charley's is no gentleman at all.

There we were with the *Lady* battered and half full of water, barely poled ashore in time to prevent her sinking, most of our smaller belongings swinging round and round in a big eddy below the chute, ourselves wet to the skin and cold beneath it, snow falling, wind blowing, ice forming, water dropping, and not one dry cigarette paper among the lot of us. Charley took a pail and started scooping water over the gunnels. Linda nursed a reluctant driftwood fire into tantalizing smoke and some small flickers of flame. I hauled my canoe out from under the fallen canvas shelter in the waist of the boat, and started bringing our small gear ashore. Suitcases, dufflebags, sleeping robes, full and empty gasoline barrels–I paddled by them all, passed everything up till I came to our fifty pound bag of flour floating lumpily on the water. I inched a line around that and towed it slowly to the beach. Charley and Linda came running, anxious. Charley cut the string. I scooped away the mess of dough at the top. Linda plunged her small hands deep into the dry flour inside and withdrew our valuables one by one: our money, Charley's great old gold watch, her passport, my scribblers, our reserve matches, and half a carton of tailor-made cigarettes. All were perfectly preserved and probably would have been safe there indefinitely. Charley's watch was still ticking. We congratulated ourselves, had a smoke, and hurried to our work again.

By the time I had the last gasoline barrel rolled up onto the beach the whole situation was considerably improved. Charley had the *Lady* floating six inches higher and was sucking the last water out of the bilge with the pump in the engine room. Linda had the fire going strongly and was stringing our wet bedding and clothes on lines around it.

She also had a pot on the fire and three tins of pork and beans warming in it. Thus did the gods set their bait before me. I was hungry, and I was getting very tired of pork and beans and I can only think my brain was as exhausted as my body..

There were inexhaustible quantities of flat limestone slabs on the beach, and there, hard by the fire, was that opened bag of flour. I stood two big rocks on their edges about two feet apart, laid another horizontally across them, and continued the same construction on a smaller scale for another story.

"Look, Charley" Linda called towards the boat. "It's happening at last. It was too much for the poor guy. He's gone nuts!"

I didn't bother to explain. They had been doubtful about that stowing of our valuables in the flour, predicting a most unholy mess. I had showed them something then, and I would show them something again. I blocked one end of my upper story, mudded the joints, got a great fire going in the lower story, and started mixing flour, water, lard, and baking powder. Linda, coming ashore with most of the engine's ignition system in her hands, found me slipping balls of dough into our frying pan.

"Bannock" I said.

"Wonderful, Ken. Come have a cigarette."

All seemed to be going well then. Charley, inventorying our goods, found that we had retrieved everything important except one gasoline barrel, which had undoubtedly gone on down river in the same direction as we would head as soon as we were ready to travel again. Linda, examining the goods, reported that hers in her suitcases had suffered much more than mine and Charley's in their duffle-bags, which was unanimously acknowledged to be a good thing, since she could better afford a loss than we could. Meantime my balls of dough were swelling to cakes and turning an appetizing brown on top.

"Mitsoo!" I called at last, "grub-pile! Victuals! Come and get it, folks!" And I was just stoking the fire for a second pan of crisp eatments when my whole oven exploded. My memory returned! The results were spectacular. "Boom!" my oven went, and hot pieces of rock hurtled through the air in all directions. Charley and Linda, fifteen feet away, were showered with small fragments, and one fairly large one hit Charley hard enough to make him drop our last tin of strawberry jam.

I was right by the oven. I got a shower of ash in my food and enough dough in my beard to keep me busy grubbing it out for half an hour afterwards. Those were trifles: Charley's gods had larger purposes than that. Two pieces of rock shot right by my face, one on either side, barely missing me. So Charley and Linda said: I remember only a whizzing in my ears. They led me up the beach and showed me one of the pieces sending up a curl of steam in the wet mud, a full ten paces from the remains of my oven. The other, they said, had gone further and plunked into the water. It was also bigger, they said.

Charley picked up the piece that lay in the mud, and hefted it. "Fifteen pounds anyways, Ken. By God! "They" nearly got you that time!"

Linda put the ignition leads back on the engine, pressed the starter, and was regarded by a few weak pops, then by a steady roar. Charley started rolling up gear, taking it aboard. I finished oiling my guns, began assembling them again, picking shells and cartridges out of their sodden cartons, slipping them into empty cans.

Linda and Charley came ashore together.

"Ready to sail?" I asked.

"I mustn't forget the fossils I saw on the beach," Linda answered. "Finish the guns, Ken. Charley and I will get them."

They wandered up the beach together, turning over the slabs of rock, Linda examining them, rejecting some, heaping others in Charley's arms till he was weighted down like a man on his way home from the liquor store. On the beach behind them, dreaming of the prospect of having my boat out of the water at Fort Simpson by that time the next day, of being soon on my way home to Barbara, I squinted idly along the sights of my .30.30.

Suddenly I stood up. The powers I had defied were relenting at last. I had packed three guns all summer and never seen anything bigger than ducks to use them on. Now I saw a caribou.

He was fording the river along the ledge of the rapids, walking, his body well above water, his head high. A following wind prevented him from smelling us, waves splashing about him prevented him from seeing us, the roar of the rapids prevented him from hearing the noise Charley and Linda were making. I waited till he was about to plunge into the Chute, to swim the last hundred feet of the ford. If I killed him here, I reasoned, he would float into the eddy below and be easy to retrieve. At the right spot I got a bead on his neck, and pulled the trigger.

"Click!" my gun went. I ejected a wet shell and took aim again. It was harder now. Sight or sound of something had frightened him, and he was headed back to the other side again, loping through the waves. Fifty yards out, he stood still momentarily, giving me another bead on his neck. I pulled the trigger. He was dead before my finger straightened again.

Instantly he began to slide down the ledge, rolling over and over, in much the same way as the *Lady* had done a few yards closer to shore two hours previously.

"He'll drift into the eddy" I said to Charley and Linda as they came running back. "I'll get him in the canoe."

It seemed a good idea. It would take a while to dress the carcass, and we might as well do so where we had the fire already going. No one then suggested going after the animal in the boat, and if anyone had I would not have agreed, because of the shallows on the edge of the eddy.

So I threw a bailer and the first piece of rope handy into the canoe and pushed off. On the far circle of the eddy I hesitated a moment. The caribou was drifting right by the eddy, in full stream, and there were some powerful little rapids just below.

Charley shouted from on shore–"Come back. We'll get him in the boat!"

There was one disadvantage to that proposal. The animal would be in the rapids before they could get underway and would follow a direct course through them, whereas the *Lady* would have to cross a full mile to the far shore to go down those rapids, then cut all the way back to this side to get in line with it again. Even with no troubles on the way, it would be getting dark before my friends reached this side again, and by then the caribou would be far downstream. Accordingly, it would be noon next day before we found him, and if he had been living on caribou moss before he died, the flesh would be quite inedible by then.

So I started paddling. I quite enjoyed the run through that first rapids. It was like old times on the Rat River again. I kept right by my animal all the way, back-paddling at times, bailing out any water I took aboard, and had the line slipped about the stubs of the caribou's horns so I could pull him ashore as soon as we reached smooth water together.

I turned the canoe then, and realized with a shock that I was much further from shore than I had intended to come. The whole thing was a trap set by Charley's gods. Fresh meat for my bean-weary stomach had been their bait this time, a dud shell and a crooked current their instruments, and the Beaver Dam they had doubtless prepared thousands of years ago for the specific purpose of giving me one final rap on the knuckles. The Beaver Dam roared a quarter of a mile below me, a straight drop of four feet anywhere I could hope to reach in it, with a madness of leaping waves and sharp pointed rocks to batter me as I shot over it.

The near shore was also about a quarter of a mile away. I started paddling towards it, letting the line attached to the horns run out till it tangled under a thwart. That saved me from making it fast, saved me a few minutes time. I was trapped, but I wasn't giving up just yet, nor surrendering my caribou either.

I have never paddled before as I paddled then. The drag kept the canoe straight; as long as I kept paddling on the same side as the line I didn't need to do any steering. I stood up on my knees and whipped my paddle in and out of the water, thrust! thrust! thrust! till my back was lead and the tendon inside my right elbow seemed on fire.

The shore drew closer. So did the Beaver Dam, roaring louder as I slid towards it. My speed forward was greater than my drift sidewise at first, till the current grew stronger. It was all very deceptive. I thought at first that I was going to make shore in safety, then realized suddenly that I wasn't. Still I paddled, angry, determined.

The shore was only ten feet from my bows now, an inviting expanse of limestone slabs. The Beaver Dam was only five feet distant. I looked over my shoulder. Insensibly, I had turned the canoe partly upstream, away from that fury of water, was paddling partly against the current. So the caribou was a few feet further downstream than I was; so he went over the Dam just as I caught sight of the him from the corner of my eye.

He went over. He dropped. He gave a tremendous pull at that snarl of rope under my thwart. The tangle gave, leaped overboard. The rope ran free, burning along my thigh. Released, my canoe shot forward to the shore.

I got my feet on the limestone slabs just as the end of the rope was slipping over the gunnel. I seized it in one hand, lifted the canoe ashore with the other, then ran down the beach till I found soft mud to dig my heels into. There I pulled in the line, hauled the caribou ashore.

I rested ten minutes before I walked back to look at the Beaver

Dam. There were some ferocious rocks in the turbulence of water close to shore. They had staved in all one side of the caribou's ribs. They would have done as much for me.

Standing there, reviewing the adventure, I think I began for the first time to accept belief in Charley's gods. "They" had set a very clever trap for me. But for a bit of luck that "they" had not counted on, "they" would have got me that time.

(So I thought then. I have revised my beliefs since. I told the story to Barbara and an admiring circle of relatives some weeks later. "Ooh!" and "Ah!" they said, and such stuff–all but little Peter.

"Mummy" he asked, "why did Daddy haff to let that wope jump fwee? Couldn't he have let it go himself?"

"Shhhh!" whispered Barbara.)

We had caribou liver for supper that night, caribou short ribs for breakfast the next morning, then took off for Simpson. Striking the Beaver Dam channel just right, we had little trouble, and were soon in good water. We caught up to our missing gasoline barrel by noon, stranded on a sand-bar, and lost two hours getting it aboard. That was well worth the trouble, but there was really no necessity at all for me to try to retrieve the old wine-bottle that I saw floating in the water as we neared Simpson Airport an hour or so later.

I was alone at the wheel at the time. Charley and Linda were forward under the canvas, packing gear. I could hear an indistinct rumble of their voices over the steady purr of the motor now and again, feel the boat rock from side to side as they moved around. When I thought of them I forgot my disappointment over the way in which my plans had gone awry. Such friends were worth more than anything the river could take from me.

That was my mood when I saw the neck of the bottle bobbing in the stream ahead of me. I had seen it similarly floating many months before, back in the hopeful days shortly after I left Fort Nelson in the *Lady* in the spring. Frenchman McGillivray Peabody had been my partner then and Frenchman had idly stabbed at the bottle with a sounding pole as we glided by it. To my surprise his aim had been perfect; to his consternation, the tip of the pole had gone true into the neck till it stuck. It was a matter of either losing the pole or gaining the bottle then. For a moment that alternative had not been quite so clear: it had seemed that we would simply lose Frenchman and the bottle. I, however, grabbed his shirt-tail just in time, and in a moment we had the bottle aboard, more of a monster than we had first counted on, a gallon thing in brown glass with a ring at its neck and a cluster of grapes in bas-relief down one side. Since then, I had packed it around all summer, thinking that it might come in useful if ever I got myself a naphtha stove for the *Lady*'s galley–if ever I built a galley in her.

That purpose was still good. I wasn't finally beaten yet. I would be down in this country another year, running my *Lady* again, living aboard her. The wine-bottle was not much, but it was something that I could save from the wreck of my fortunes.

The same sounding pole was in its holder beside the pilot-house door. I yanked it out, throttled down slightly, and leaned far overboard. The little *Lady* heeled as I leaned, and Charley, moving something heavy forward, fell with it against the starboard side, making the boat heel farther yet. I was holding onto the jamb of the pilot-house door with one hand. The pilot-house, a rickety enough affair when I first built it, had been severely strained when we rolled over in the rapids the day before. The whole thing began to come away in my hand. It was obvious then that I was going overboard, but at the moment I saw no sense in taking the pilot-house with me. I let go.

After the first brief surprise-panic, I wasn't afraid. I thought I was quite calm even; but I wasn't. The proof of that is that instead of at once striking out for the nearest shore, I started floundering along in the same direction as the boat was going, following it. Practically, that was a matter of no significance whatever: with my kind of swimming it made no material difference to my chances of survival no matter which way I pointed myself. That water was cold, very near freezing. Ice was forming in all the quiet bays along the shore. I doubt whether any man could have swum ashore in that water. My only chance was to keep afloat till I was carried to a shallows or till Linda and Charley noticed my absence and came back to pick me up.

I had taken in a little water when I first went overboard, and was perturbed about it. I was more perturbed about my boots, heavy laced rubber leather-tops. All I had ever read of other men in such predicaments indicated that the first thing I ought to do was to kick off my boots. Some men I had read of would have had them off almost as soon as they hit the water. Accordingly, I tried to take off

142

my boots, feeling very calm and professional about the whole thing. Unfortunately, nothing I had ever read explained how the trick was done. I worked at them for about five minutes, then gave up. The only result of that attempt was that I had taken in a little more water and began to know a little fear.

My legs and arms were growing numb. The picture of myself that I got was like that of one of those fat white comic-book ghosts who float in the air with their extremities dwindling away to vague points. Somewhere in my vicinity my hands and feet were still thrashing away, but my connection with them was becoming increasingly tenuous.

The *Lady* still plugged long downstream, fair in the channel, a good half-mile from me now. Sooner or later she would strike a bar or run into ricky shallows, causing Linda and Charley to pop their heads out from under the canvas to see whether I needed help. They would soon see that I did; but it was slowly coming to me that by the time they realized what new sort of help I needed I would be beyond it.

They say that when a man first realises he is drowning, he gets a quick flash-back of all the life he has lived, from minute events of childhood onwards. As far as I am concerned, that story goes on the shelf with the one about the quickly kicked-off boots. I did have a crowded mental picture of the past, it is true, but the time was limited to the events of that summer. My first adventure into the North by this route, the simple plans I had had then, the complications I had become involved in, the money I had hoped to make, the money I had not made, the accidents I had had–in a hazy jumble they passed through my mind, leaving me no clear impression but that I had got a very raw deal. I had worked hard. I had tried hard. Other fellows at times had said that I was quite intelligent. And everything, right to this last moment, everything had gone wrong.

I also saw some distance into the future. Often when thinking about death I had felt that my chief desideratum was to go out cleanly, leaving all my affairs in order. That wasn't the way I was going out at all. I still owed money on the boat, and the boat itself was a mass of unknown value unknown miles from anywhere in which such value as it had could be realized. Charley and Linda, who had done so much for me already, would see to getting it out of the water for me, but who, next year, would attend to the selling of it?

143

Who would see that Barbara got a fair price on this relic of my hopes? Would she even get enough to pay off what I still owed Jack Havens on it?

Then the worst thought of all came to my mind. If Charley and Linda didn't start looking for me soon, they might never find me. The ice would come, ending the search. The ice would go, next spring, leaving very little to be found. There would be no proof of my death. At times during the summer adventures it had been comforting to think that my life was insured. It wasn't comforting now. It might be seven years before Barbara could collect the money.

That was the last hopeless muddle of the life I had wished, when the time came, to end cleanly. That was the climax of the whole wretched, annoying summer. It wasn't fair, the way I had been treated. I don't think I was afraid; but I remember being very annoyed. I could have cried. I didn't. Instead: "Oh, damn it!" I said.

Those, I suppose, would have been my last words if it had not been for that wine bottle. I had given up my hopeless attempt to overtake the *Lady* and had floundered about to splash toward the sounding pole which had come overboard with me. It might help a little, I thought.

The bottle, deeper in the water, moved faster downstream than the pole. I had quite forgotten it. My eyes fixed on the foot-long ring of brilliant colour on the pole. I did not notice the bottle's neck until it was bobbing a few inches in front of my nose.

A drowning man, they say, will grasp at a straw. It is accordingly no reflection on my character that I laid eager hands on that wine bottle.

It was nearly full by then, nearly foundered by the splash I made when I fell into the water beside it. It had bare buoyancy left to keep its rim afloat. Its state was really more desperate than mine. It sank instantly when I seized it, emitting one melancholy "burp."

I had one finger through the glass ring on its neck. I raised it out of the water, turned it on its side.

"Glug, glug, glug" it went.

Then "glug, glug, glug" went I. I hadn't thought of that. As it went up I went down. I was caught by surprise the first time and, hastily thrusting it into the water again, lost all I had gained. Bubbles rising from its neck slapped me about the face.

I let my feet drop, took a long breath, and again lifted the bottle, bottom up. Down below, holding my breath, I felt it lurch gently in my hands, giving a sort of little kick every time the flow ceased and air came in. This time when I pulled it down and myself up again, I pulled the neck down first. Already it was a help. I rested a while, then tried again. On the fifth try, the little lurches ceased abruptly, the bottle was empty. The whole Imperial gallon, ten pounds avoirdupois, had run out. My whole head could not weigh much more than that.

I hooked my right arm through my belt, hooked my right forefinger through the ring on the bottle, clamped my left hand over the right forefinger, and struggled no more.

In that position, about half an hour later, Charley and Linda found me. They said it took them three minutes to persuade me to let go the bottle. They said that at first they thought they were too late. Linda said I was damn smart to hang onto that bottle. Charley said I was damn lucky–this time and all the other times when I came out of near disasters with barely a scratch. Charley said "they" must have been looking after me–and he said a lot more–unrepeatable here. But then as I said at the beginning, it should be Charley telling this story, not me.

Charley and Linda took the *Lady* into Simpson's float-plane Airport, and finding a crew of Department of Transport men moving gas-barrels on the beach, in about ten minutes had me wrapped in blankets in one of the administration buildings beside the runways. By the time they let me out of the blankets again, the D.O.T. men had hauled my boat out on shore behind a bulldozer, safe for the winter. A cable broke during the hauling, whipping somebody's hat off his head; but that was clearly a mistake, since at the time I was sitting up to sip hot broth a full mile away. I appreciated the fact that "they" realised their error in time to remove a hat rather than a head.

The D.O.T. men were mighty good to us all, and when we thanked them, merely replied: "Hell! You pay taxes, don't you?"

They appreciated the caribou meat, and doubtless appreciated Linda's company still more. Charley and I shared the guest cabin; Linda bunked in with one of the stenographers. And we all grew very tired of waiting for a plane to take us out of the country.

Linda's attitude was curious. She had never before shown the least annoyance at the numerous delays we had suffered. Now she threw

145

her weight and her lipstick around in a way that neither Simpson nor its airport will forget in a hurry, sending wires, receiving wires, grumbling continually. Finally, on the very day Charley and I had completed what work we felt it necessary to do on the boat before we left, she greeted us with the announcement that she refused to wait for the scheduled flight and had chartered a small plane to come specially from the south to take her back to civilisation. Just a small plane, she said, but it was larger than she needed for herself, and if we happened to know of a couple of fellows anxious to shake Liard mud off their feet and return to home-cooking again, she knew of no reason why they should not accompany her.

We offered to pay her regular fare, of course, but she went all of a tremble at the mere thought of that. There was some law, she explained, forbidding sub-letting on planes, and she, being a foreigner and all, had to be very careful about that sort of thing. It wasn't any use arguing with her.

It was a nice enough little plane, if you like planes, and had the advantage of a following wind all the way from Simpson south, a great gusty wind carrying our wintry weather with us. We left Simpson airport at nine in the morning, stopped at McMurray to refuel, and were nearing Edmonton by dusk. I had just finished telling stories of other adventures I had experienced that summer.

"What a time you've had this summer!" Linda exclaimed. "But you're safe now, Ken. Look. Lights."

I leaned over her shoulder to peer through the window beside her. There indeed were the lights of the city at last, lines and lines of them in orderly rows below us. Order, arrangement, security, was the message they winked up at me. Down there, my kind went to office or store or factory in the morning, worked so many hours, returned at night exactly on the minute to the safety of their homes. It was a dull life they led, perhaps, but it had the advantage of security. You were safe there; you always knew what was going to happen next.

The plane dipped, zoomed, b-r-r-r-ed, and performed the other antics of its kind. Give me a canoe and paddle every time.

"Fast water here" said Charley.

The wheels touched ground, bumped, and touched again.

"Sandbar" said Charley.

We rolled to the door of the reception room. Linda was first out, then myself, Charley passing out baggage behind us. Good hard

146

pavement with just a trace of snow on it was under my feet, hard, solid, unyielding concrete laid by men for men to walk on. I stamped on it delightedly. I was safe now.

I didn't help with the baggage. I had spotted Barbara and the children waiting by the big doorway, Peter gazing with great interest at a little red rubber-tired baggage-puller, John pointing towards me, wide-eyed at the sight of this disgorgement of bearded men from the shining body of the plane, Barbara paying no attention to the boys, gazing at me with a shining and shyness in her eyes. I hurried towards them.

"It's the wind from the north" said the airport major-domo apologetically. "Ice first, then snow on top of it. Whole city slippery as—Oooops! there, I nearly went down—slippery as hell."

"It's been following us all day" said Charley. "Same damn wind been following us all the way from Aklavik in fact." He bent over me.

"Ken, darling, my darling! said Barbara. "No, no, don't try to get up. They'll be here with the stretcher in a moment." And she put her arms about me, holding me close.

So the stretcher came.

"Be careful with him, men" said Linda. "I think he's broken his leg."

I had too.

EPILOGUE

Death of the *Lady Greenbelly*

I never did sell the *Lady Greenbelly*. Nobody in Aklavik, or anywhere else, wanted anything to do with her as she limped along on her misshapen propeller. The only profitable deal I ever got out of her was that load of five tons of coal we moved from Aklavik to Tuktoyaktuk. She then took Bill and Jack and me to the mouth of the Husky Channel, waited there for my return from helping them up the Rat River on their way to the Bell River and their eventual return by canoe and plane to their home in Seattle. Then there began that series of adventures I had in the *Lady* between Aklavik and Fort Simpson. Being unable to make any headway on the Liard, I got the *Lady Greenbelly* hauled out at Fort Simpson Airport and flew out from there to Edmonton.

The next spring, 1947, conscious of that $1600 or more I had tied up in that craft, I took a canoe on the train to Fort Nelson, paddled it down to Fort Simpson, and there gave the *Lady* a proper propeller. After many unsuccessful attempts to sell her in Fort Simpson, Providence, Hay River, Resolution, and Fort Smith, (her history was too well-known throughout the North) I got her hauled out in the Bell Rock shipyards eight miles downriver from Fort Smith. The next year, 1948, I rowed a skiff from Fort McMurray to Fort Fitzgerald (about 300 miles), got the *Lady Greenbelly* launched at Bell Rock, took her down to Hay River, where commercial fishing had begun just the year before, and used her, with some success, as a fish boat.

Her engine by then required some overhauling. With the help of a better mechanic than I was, we lifted the engine out of the boat, set it safely ashore, ground the valves, and left it there for the winter. In the meantime I had got her hull to one of the islands near the mouth of the Hay, hauled it as far ashore as I could with block and tackle, tied it to several large trees, and so left it for the winter. In the spring of 1949, an ice jam formed across the mouth of the Hay, the water rose rapidly, *Lady Greenbelly* broke loose from her mooring, was carried out onto the lake, and, I was told by my Hay River friends, several times almost made it back into the river, carried by winds and currents, before she was finally carried away by those same winds and currents. I never saw her again, though I think I may have stumbled on some broken bits of her wreckage some years later when walking the shoreline from Hay River to West Channel.

So died the *Lady Greenbelly*, but her engine remained, a valuable item, valuable enough to draw me North again in subsequent summers. I used it in 1949 as the sole engine in *Splash*, a boat which I bought from a sawmill that had gone bankrupt on the Slave River. *Splash* was equipped for two engines, but did well enough on one to transport large quantities of lumber from the mill to Hay River. The next year, 1950, I got another V8 engine, installed it, and went into the fish-hauling business on Great Slave Lake, sometimes in *Splash*, sometimes in company boats, which kept me busy in the North every summer until the spring of 1958, when I got a job in Vancouver that required me all the year around.

That same year I sold both the *Lady Greenbelly*'s V8 engine and the newer V8 engine to one of the fish companies in Hay River. So, thank God, ended all my last connections with the ill-fated (and sometimes, I think, malevolent) *Lady Greenbelly*.

About the Author

"The Kipling of the North"

Kenneth Conibear was born in Canada in 1907, and moved with his family to the Northwest Territories in 1912, travelling there by rail, stagecoach and barge. He was raised in Fort Smith, and was home-educated to the grade 10 level by his parents and friends within that community. He was sent out to Edmonton to complete grades 11 and 12, and continued on to the University of Alberta where he was selected as the Alberta Rhodes Scholar in 1931. Following 3 years at Oxford, he spent the next three years in England writing and had his first novel, the highly acclaimed "Northland Footprints" published in 1936. It was then that he was referred to as 'the Kipling of the North'. In 1937 his publisher, Lovat Dickson, hired him to travel with and manage the Canadian Indian naturalist Grey Owl's speaking tour of England, and he has often been consulted as an expert on Grey Owl. In 1938 he returned to the Northwest Territories with his wife, Barbara, and had "Northward to Eden" published, followed in 1940 by the novel, "Husky" written in collaboration with his brother, Frank, and "The Nothing Man," privately published in 1995. In the north, he was a hunter, trapper, storekeeper and skipper of his own fish-packing/freight boat. All of these novels were based on his intimate knowledge and love of the people, the animals, and the natural environment of the north. He presently lives in Vancouver, British Columbia with his second wife, Marilyn.